Extreme SEA KAYAKING

ERIC SOARES AND MICHAEL POWERS

Ragged Mountain Press • McGraw-Hill

Camden, Maine • New York • San Francisco • Washington, D.C. • Auckland • Bogotá • Caracas • Lisbon • London • Madrid • Mexico City • Milan • Montreal • New Delhi • San Juan • Singapore • Sydney • Tokyo • Toronto

Ragged Mountain Press

A Division of The **McGraw·Hill** Companies

10 9 8 7 6 5 4 3 2 1

Copyright © 1999 Ragged Mountain Press

All rights reserved. The publisher takes no responsibility for the use of any of the materials or methods described in this book, nor for the products thereof. The name "Ragged Mountain Press" and the Ragged Mountain Press logo are trademarks of The McGraw-Hill Companies. Printed in the United States of America.

Library of Congress Cataloging-in-Publication Data
Soares, Eric J.
  Extreme sea kayaking / Eric Soares and Michael Powers.
   p. cm.
  Includes bibliographical references (p.) and index.
  ISBN 0-07-050718-X
  1. Sea Kayaking. I. Powers, Michael, 1940 Aug. 10– II. Title.
GV788.5.S63 1999
797. 1'224—dc21   99-10718
               CIP

Questions regarding the content of this book should be addressed to
Ragged Mountain Press
P.O. Box 220
Camden, ME 04843
www.raggedmountainpress.com

Questions regarding the ordering of this book should be addressed to
The McGraw-Hill Companies
Customer Service Department
P.O. Box 547
Blacklick, OH 43004
Retail customers: 1-800-262-4729
Bookstores: 1-800-722-4726

This book is printed on 70-pound Citation.
Printed by Quebecor Printing, Fairfield, PA
All photos by Michael Powers unless otherwise credited
Design by Susan Newman Design, Inc.
Production by Deborah Evans and Dan Kirchoff
Edited by Tom McCarthy, Jane Curran, and D. A. Oliver

Gore-Tex, Jacuzzi, Kevlar, Lexan, and Velcro are registered trademarks

Warning: Sea kayaking can take paddlers into harm's way, exposing them to risks of injury, cold-water exposure and hypothermia, drowning, and other hazards that can lead to serious injury or death. Extreme sea kayaking activities discussed in this book heighten those risks and are potentially lethal.

  This book is not intended to replace instruction by a qualified teacher or to substitute for good personal judgment. In using this book, the reader releases the authors, publisher, and distributor from liability for any injury, including death, that might result. It is understood that you paddle at your own risk.

Contents

Foreword

It seems many years ago now since I first heard of the Tsunami Rangers. I had been running some ocean kayaking classes for a friend of mine in Sausalito, just north of San Francisco. I had been in California for a while, and it was time for me to return to my teaching post back in England. As I remember, I was busy packing my bags when I was asked if I would like to go and watch a slide presentation. I wasn't excited by the offer, because over the years I have sat through numerous slide shows and been bored silly more times than I can remember. I suppose I've become blasé to the things people can do in kayaks. It was with some reluctance, therefore, that I agreed to attend this one, which was to be given by Eric Soares. I had to confess that I had never heard of the Tsunami Rangers, and when I asked what they did, I was told vaguely, "I think these guys do things in surf!"

I had "discovered" the California surf in the early 1980s. For an Englishman used to surfing on the North Sea coast, teaching kayak surfing classes on California "beaches" was a dream come true. It wasn't long, however, before I learned what the shores of the Pacific Ocean could inflict on the unwary.

We had paddled 15 miles down northern California's Lost Coast of Mendocino. It had been a warm summer's day, but now it was time for me and my group to find a landing place and pitch camp for the night. While we had been paddling offshore down the coast, I hadn't noticed just how big the swells were. Close into shore, however, the waves that were thundering and dumping onto the steeply sloping beach were enough to give anyone nightmares. My idea was simple enough: we would find a way in through the rocks that guarded the beach; then I would get close in and make sure that a landing was possible. Once on shore, I would bring the others in one at a time and then pull them safely up onto the beach. That was the plan.

Threading our way in-between the network of offshore rocks was no problem. Then it was my turn to paddle in alone as near to the shore as possible and wait for a chance to land. I must have sat for about 20 minutes just outside the surf line, waiting for a lull in-between the huge sets. I constantly looked over my shoulder, getting more and more uneasy. Then, just when I thought we would have to sit there all night, I thought I detected a break in the lethal hydraulics. Since the surf didn't look as if it were going to get any lower, I accelerated toward the beach. I say "accelerated," but just when speed was essential, my loaded kayak felt like a lump of lead on the water. It was then that things started to go wrong.

I sensed, rather than saw, the dark, towering shadow that came creeping up behind me. As I half-turned, I saw that the steep wave face had caught up with me. I felt the boat twist sideways and rise up the steep wall. I seemed to be looking down on the beach and knew I had to get rid of my boat. I don't think I've ever exited from a kayak as quickly in my life. I came out of the cockpit and pushed the boat away from me in one quick movement. Then, suddenly, together with lots of weed, driftwood of various sizes, and a kayak weighing 150 pounds, I was pitched over the falls.

I must have landed headfirst in about 4 feet of water. Even though my fall had been cushioned by the water, I hit my head hard on the bottom and ground my face into the sand. At first, I wasn't sure whether I'd broken my neck, my nose, or a couple of ribs. By a stroke of good fortune, the kayak had missed me by about 3 feet.

I managed to grab my boat and haul it to safety, just as we were both being rolled back down the steep slope by the receding foam. Then I sat down on the beach, with sand and grit up my nose and in my mouth, feeling as if I'd been in a road accident. It was the last wave of the day!

As the lecture hall darkened, I whispered, "What do you mean, they *do things* in surf?"

"I'm not sure," came the response, "but I think they play in big surf amongst the rocks and inside the caves."

With my own experience of California surf, this I had to see! And I did. I sat with sweating palms and in stunned silence for over an hour, looking at images of boats and human beings being thrashed by surf in among rock gardens and engulfed by foam in the claustrophobic darkness of sea caves. "They're lunatics," I whispered, but I couldn't hide my admiration.

I felt they had been wise to use specially designed surf skis and not kayaks for their work in the surf. The kayak paddler is enclosed by a cockpit and is committed to the boat. An exit means that a boat has to be emptied and reentered, and this requires assistance. Sit-on-tops and surf skis, on the other hand, do not have these problems.

The young man who delivered the talk was pleasant to listen to and had a gentle sense of humor. He sounded quite normal, and I wondered what on earth prompted him to take what I considered such awful risks. I didn't have to wait long to find out. When he finished the slides, the lights went up, and he came forward to say a few words in conclusion. I couldn't believe my ears as I heard him mention my name and thank me for writing the book from which he had gained his inspiration.

So why do some people put themselves voluntarily at risk for the sake of recreation? Does it really refresh their spirits? Is it merely for thrills? Why do some people put themselves into frightening positions in order to get the adrenaline rush or perhaps merely the satisfaction of overcoming the predicament and the fear that they brought upon themselves in the first place? Kayakers jump waterfalls, descend "impossible" rivers, and cross open seas in solo kayaks. When every other animal looks for the easy way across a river or the pass between the mountains, why should human beings be different? What kind of mutation of the human spirit compels people to take what at first appears to be meaningless risks?

In his excellent book *The Ulysses Factor*, J. R. L. Anderson takes the anthropological approach and states, "there is some factor in man, some special form of adaptation, which prompts a few individuals to exploits which, however purposeless they may seem, are of value to the survival of the human race. . . . adaptation takes many forms, and since we cannot see the end product of human evolution, we cannot know to what new strains and stresses man may have to adapt."

It is good to know that the spirit of Ulysses is alive and well in the Tsunami Rangers. Long may they pursue their own personal road to Valhalla.

—Derek C. Hutchinson
South Shields, U.K.

Acknowledgments

> "Let the beauty
> we love be
> what we do."
> –Rumi

This book would never have been written were it not for our fellow Tsunami Rangers, who share fully in the adventure, teach us by example, and live the power of the tribe. We especially thank Jim Kakuk, our captain, for being a fountain of wisdom and leadership. Special thanks also go to commander John Lull for critiquing parts of the manuscript and for his numerous suggestions.

A Tsunami salute to our literary sea daddy, Derek Hutchinson, whose love of adventure and the sea has inspired us and many others. Gracias, Padre Jack Izzo, S.J., for serving as our chaplain and possessing the faith to go out kayaking with us. We learned a lot about the history and philosophy of sea kayaking from George Dyson, Will Nordby, Jim Berta, and Paul Kaufmann. Andy Taylor and Steve Sinclair of Force Ten were wellsprings of information about storm paddling, rescues, and safety. Dave and John Nagle and the other Banzai Bozos enlivened many ocean episodes with their warm camaraderie and can-do spirit. We also thank Ken Fink, John Dowd, and Bea Dowd for being our advocates.

Eric fondly remembers his father, John, for sharing his love of the water and teaching him how to swim, canoe, and sail. He also thanks his siblings, Marc, Camille, and John, for continuing childhood adventures well into adulthood, and his mother, Mozelle, for allowing her son to dance to a different drumbeat. Michael will always remember his grandfather building a wooden boat one winter in northern Idaho and taking him and brother Pat out on the flood-swollen Pend Oreille River in the spring.

The Inuits believed that as long as they remembered to bring the warmth of their women to their kayaks each time they prepared to go hunting in the sea, the boats would possess great power and always bear them safely back to land. We thank our loving wives, Nancy and Nani, for giving freely of their warmth, and also for joining us for some of those grand adventures in the sea.

We remain in awe of those early kayakers who braved northern waters for millennia before us, evolving paddling and boat building skills still practiced by modern sea kayakers. Finally, we look forward to the great deeds kayakers will do in the next thousand years.

Bold Ventures beyond the Shore

> " There is no scale to rate the difficulty of ocean kayaking; it is not an exact sport. Mostly we experiment, sometimes without prior example, but always with an open mind. There is never a second when we are not learning. "
> —Captain Jim Kakuk, Tsunami Rangers

What is *extreme* sea kayaking? It's kayaking on the outermost edges of the ocean; to go farther is to fall off the face of the earth and into the abyss. It's sea kayaking taken to the greatest degree, at its most radical, advanced, drastic. It's akin to whitewater river kayaking in its challenge and appeal. It could also be called ocean *whitewater* kayaking or ocean *adventure* kayaking. It takes courage, physical ability, a keen mind, and years of training to become proficient. It is always changing and evolving, always on the outside of the envelope. It is done in extreme conditions—big waves, heavy weather, surf zones, rock gardens, and sea caves.

Extreme sea kayaking differs from modern bluewater sea kayaking in many ways. The table below contrasts the two approaches, showing a general representation of two types of experienced sea kayakers.

These ten factors illustrate opposite poles of sea kayaking. In reality, few paddlers would consider themselves

Types of Kayakers

Normal-Condition Kayakers

1. Prefer flat water
2. Paddle straight-tracking kayaks designed for comfort and stability
3. Are lean, with good stamina
4. Are objective, strategic
5. Paddle smoothly, efficiently
6. Paddle from point A to point B; explore, launch, and land in protected areas
7. Are navigators, comfortable *on* the water
8. Are good planners
9. Tend to be conservative, sensible
10. Are solo or group-oriented

Extreme-Condition Kayakers

1. Prefer whitewater
2. Paddle shorter, stronger kayaks designed for high performance
3. Are athletic, with good coordination
4. Are intuitive, tactical
5. Paddle skillfully, effectively
6. Paddle surf and rock gardens; explore, launch, and land along remote, rugged coasts
7. Are wave warriors, happy *in* the water
8. Are good operators
9. Tend to be bold, risk-taking
10. Are team-oriented

fitting predominantly in one column or the other. It is better to view items on the list as a continuum, with most people falling somewhere along it. Ideally, you will recognize aspects of yourself in both categories. Fun-loving, reasonably adventurous kayakers would paddle different boats for different purposes, improve their stamina and coordination, be strategic and tactical, be good *on* and *in* the water, be a planner and an operator, be cautiously bold, go solo and with a team. The objective is not to categorize and thus limit yourself but to be eager to learn and receptive to new experiences. *Openness* is the ticket for experienced sea kayakers who want to experiment with the wilder side and for those new to sea kayaking who are curious about the best approach to take to the comprehensive activity known as sea kayaking.

Many people know what comprises normal sea kayaking—safely paddling in somewhat protected waters during periods of calm. A dozen books tell you how, what, when, where, and why. The purpose of this book is to depict what is entailed in extreme sea kayaking and to describe

how to do it as safely as possible. In brief, extreme sea kayaking encompasses the following: kayak surfing, storm kayaking, touring the exposed coast, playing in ocean rock gardens, and exploring sea caves. To get through such potentially lethal activities relatively unscathed, you must possess specialized knowledge and skills. This book will help you attain knowledge without the incumbent pain associated with trial and error.

It's important to state at the outset that the only way to learn how to paddle in extreme conditions is to go out there and do it, in increments, with skilled teachers. That said, you can use this book to augment your forays in the wild sea. The book contains suggestions on what to look for (and look out for), what to do in certain situations, and how to best prepare yourself. It is prescriptive, based on our experiences in the school of wild waves and hard rocks. Our opinions are our own and may be at odds with those of established sea kayaking gurus. So be it. We do not give short shrift to the danger that abounds, for to do so would encourage you to ignore hazards and to risk getting caught unawares. We believe it is far better to face reality squarely, for only then can you adequately adjust to the situation and make the right moves.

Whether you are contemplating your first paddle in the ocean or are already an experienced sea kayaker, the fact that you picked up a book on *extreme* sea kayaking means you have an adventurous streak inside you that yearns to risk the unknown, in the ever changing, restless, chaotic, scary but alluring ocean. Sometimes, reading anecdotes about the sea lets us vicariously experience what is out there and inspires us to try it ourselves. Read Michael Powers's story on what it's like amid ocean whitewater, and imagine yourself out there with us.

Exploits like these by the Tsunami Rangers, Force Ten, the Banzai Bozos, and other storm-surf paddling teams occurred along rugged stretches of coastline and in tempestuous weather, beyond the gaze of shore-based observers. Still, reports of dangerous, high-adrenaline sea kayaking incidents continued to circulate among the ocean paddling community. Back in the mid-1980s, the Rangers began holding extreme-condition sea kayaking races along particularly notorious stretches of the northern California coastline. Paddlers traveled from as far away as the Atlantic coast and Russia to participate. These races, started by Force Ten in the early 1980s, consisted of surf launches and landings and grueling 7-mile sprints through breakers and around sea stacks.

A minor setback happened when the American Canoe Association saw an early video of the Rangers in action and promptly canceled our race insurance. Since officials insisted that events held on state beaches

A Pack of Wild Dogs

Like the sun breaking through the clouds during that final pitch to a mountain summit, there are pinnacles in extreme-condition sea kayaking that are never forgotten. One was a midwinter morning on the Big Sur coast when our kayaking team, the Tsunami Rangers, paddled coastal waters seething with epic storm swells. The Rangers, searching for a safe place to land, had spotted a tiny beach glimmering between the sheer cliffs looming along the rugged shore. But getting there demanded crossing a half-submerged reef where big waves lunged and broke, rebounded, and fought among themselves like a pack of wild dogs. The whole reef seemed to tremble beneath the fierce attack and roared continuously. Then, for a moment, the onslaught of waves at their backs seemed to lessen. At a signal from our leader, we charged into the whitewater that stood between us and shore. But progress through this labyrinth of convulsive, heaving seas and landmine-like rocks proved treacherous and agonizingly slow.

Sensing time had run out, Commander Eric Soares stole a furtive glance over his shoulder. "Outside!" he bellowed. Everyone spun their boats around and raced back toward deeper water, but it was too late. A colossal wave had risen to form a translucent green wall, two stories high. Eric, deepest in the smash zone, was directly in the path of this man-eater. "Holy shibooty!" he gasped. The wave arched over him and collapsed, burying him and his kayak beneath tons of water.

After a few long, terrible moments, the golden nose of Eric's Tsunami X-1 Rocket Boat burst to the surface again. The enormous energy of the breaking wave had ejected the kayak from its depths and sent it flying, clear out of the water. For a heart-stopping moment, Soares and his sleek craft hung motionless in the sky before going into free fall.

Then there was the time Captain Jim Kakuk, most senior officer of the Rangers, deliberately surfed his X-1 into Sniveler's Slit. Dreaded Sniveler's Slit is a gigantic cleft worn deep into Mesozoic granite on the northern California coast. No sane kayaker had

Michael Powers surfs in front of his home at Miramar Beach. A waterproof camera was attached to the bow of his kayak.

ever gone there before, nor probably ever will again. Kakuk paid for the privilege by nearly biting the big one when he was caught by a rogue wave and hurtled head first, straight into a jagged stone wall. Luckily, the crash helmet and ninja face shield he was wearing saved his handsome features from too serious a rearrangement.

—Michael Powers

be insured, we were forced to seek out more remote, un-regulated locations in which to launch our races.

Meanwhile, talks and slide shows on extreme-condition paddling were receiving enthusiastic responses at sea kayaking clubs and symposia. Stories appeared in magazines and newspapers with increasing frequency. Photographers, journalists, filmmakers from *National Geographic Explorer*, ESPN, MTV Sports, and the Discovery Channel made documentaries on extreme-ocean kayaking for broadcast on national television. Storm surfing and exploration of rock gardens and sea caves by kayak began gaining notoriety, albeit as lunatic-fringe, high-risk sport activities.

especially when we paddled along wilderness shorelines on long exploratory trips. Landing on remote, pristine beaches, we often lingered around a fire at night, reveling in the peace and unhurried freedom of the nomadic sea kayaking way of life. At these times, the spirit of ancient hunter-gatherers felt very strong. Perhaps they had once huddled together on these very beaches, gazing out hungrily over seas that seethed with game. We imagined the hunter who had labored to stretch and sew scraps of skin over a crude framework of driftwood and bone, holding up the first primitive baidarka for others to admire.

Kayak surfing champion Beth Borgeson waits for a break in the confused seas to plow her way outside.

Still, those of us who love dancing among rocks and waves in our kayaks knew we were doing nothing new. The courageous and resourceful coastal peoples who built the first baidarkas (sealskin boats) and began venturing into fearsome northern seas long ago were the true vanguard of our sport. We felt a deep kinship with them,

Following the lead of those early sea venturers, we discovered that modern versions of their swift, maneuverable crafts could bear us, too, out into that mysterious, exquisite world beyond the shore. The only limitations we encountered there were those imposed by our own strength, skill, and courage. We paid our dues in the surf zone, getting capsized, pounded around by breaking waves, and cast back unceremoniously onto the beach. Boats got sucked into rock gardens and broken in half. One day at Pillar Point, next to infamous Mavericks Break, a brand-new Tsunami-designed kayak was torn from the grasp of Haruo Hasegawa, the Ranger cadet who had built it, and was swept away, never to be seen again. Cameras and other coveted gear also got broken or lost. Yet, measured against the joy and excitement of our adventures in the sea, the tributes we paid seemed small.

We began exploring stretches of nearly inaccessible, seldom seen coast, honing our skills in increasingly challenging conditions. Ocean kayaking in big winds and waves meant literally living life a bit beyond the edge and upon the most visceral of terms. Admittedly, the risks were part of the rush. The sound of the surf thundering in our ears, the bite of the sea air in our faces, and the current surging beneath our boats were primal and powerful, just as they must have been for those first courageous paddlers.

Tsunami Rangers mix it up in the surf at Martin's Beach.

Our encounters with other living creatures in the sea were memorable and oftentimes deeply moving experiences. Just as their baidarkas empowered the aboriginal sea hunters to pursue their quarry as never before, we discovered that the ability to move swiftly and silently around the marine environment brought us into intimate contact with the wild things that dwelled there.

Migrating gray whales surfaced unexpectedly, sometimes so close to us that we gazed straight into their huge eyes. Brown pelicans, master flyers who surfed the air currents inches above the sea, rose suddenly when our plunging kayaks flushed schools of sardines to the surface, and hurtled back down like dive-bombers into the midst of their prey. Silver-pelted sea otters floated on their backs among the kelp beds and feasted on delicacies plucked from the rocky bottom, while gulls hovered overhead, eager for any scrap of sushi the otters might disregard. Off the coasts of northern California and southern Chile, we were filled with wonder when immense flocks of sooty shearwaters filled summer skies and descended to blanket the surface of the sea around us. Paddling around Kodiak Island in the Gulf of Alaska, we gave wide berth to the massive brown bears that lumbered out of the emerald forest to feast on spawning salmon. In the ice-choked fjords of Norway's Spitsbergen archipelago, 900 miles north of the European continent, we had to carry guns and set explosive alarms around our tents to protect ourselves from hungry polar bears. On South Georgia Island in Antarctica, we paddled into coves where vast colonies of penguins dotted the landscape as far as we could see and territorial fur seals chased us off the beach when we attempted to land.

Back in California, we marveled at the grace and power of the sea lions we encountered in the breaking surf along the volatile outer fringes of offshore reef zones. They would erupt from the top of waves, rocket down the vertical faces, and vanish beneath our boats. We learned, however, never to drift between a big bull sea lion and his escape route back to the sea, once he had clambered up on an exposed reef. To do so was to risk being trampled if he decided to charge suddenly, grizzly-like, back toward deep water.

"I like to think, though, that in modern replicas of the 'hunter's boat' we can keep the skills and some of the spirit alive." —Derek C. Hutchinson senior coach, British Canoe Union

The Evolution of Sea Kayaking

Extreme-condition sea kayaking developed in response to pragmatic human needs, to hunt and gather living sustenance for food and clothing. Though those instincts remain strong, most of us are drawn to the sea today by somewhat different motives. Folks of adventuresome nature are returning to the waterways of the planet, drawn by hunger of the spirit, not of the belly. Whether for a few hours or an extended expedition, we slip away from shore and move quietly along a rugged wilderness coast. Out to sea in a kayak, we find that life in the crowded twentieth century is easily forgotten. We pass by, and not a footstep or footprint, not a trace of our passing, remains behind. Water slips soundlessly past our boats. The sandpiper settles back upon her rock. Beyond the kayak's bow, oncoming waves stretch endlessly to the horizon, kelp forests sway in harmony with eternal rhythms, sea caves beckon, and other living creatures, some much larger and more powerful than ourselves, move about freely.

Sea kayaking in extreme conditions, like mountain climbing, evolved out of necessity. Alexander the Great didn't order his troops to climb the sheer cliffs of the impregnable Rock of Sogdiana at night for fun but to conquer the Bactrian Oxyartes. Early coastal peoples paddled out in stormy seas, not for recreation, but to hunt or to escape from attack by marauding invaders.

Technique and equipment have evolved dramatically in sea kayaking over the past 30 years, just as they have for other outdoor sport activities. Just a few years ago, it may have taken heavily laden climbers days to climb a big wall like Yosemite's Half Dome. Now, free climbers scramble to impressive heights with minimal high-tech equipment in an afternoon. Modern recreational sea kayaking, which began in the Pacific Northwest and Great Britain, has grown immensely popular and has spread worldwide. Until recently, the emphasis was on bluewater touring and its associated skills; kayak surfing, rock garden and sea cave exploration, and other forms of extreme-condition paddling were only engaged in by an esoteric few. Today, increasing numbers of paddlers are pushing the outer edge of the sea kayaking spectrum and enhancing their paddling skills.

In the 1400s, Europeans still believed that the earth was flat. Sailing beyond the horizon was to risk falling off the edge of the world and was considered foolhardy. But a few brave souls dared to sail beyond that imaginary edge and discovered a rich new world. We hope that *Extreme Sea Kayaking* will introduce you to vast new realms of personal experience and adventure on the wild, outer edges of the water planet.

Just as a culture evolves, so can an individual. Educated people know that the earth is not flat; it's a geoid. Many people today are beginning to realize that the seascape painting of storm-tossed waves hitting a rocky shoreline is not a forbidden zone to kayakers. You *can* put yourself in the painting. All it takes is opening yourself to learning about and loving water. The process takes a lifetime but is well worth it, since much of the surface of this spherical world is covered by the sea yet is unexplored. Read the story of how Eric Soares evolved in his understanding of and interaction with the water planet. Then, think about your own relationship with the sea, how it developed, and where it will go next.

The Journey Ahead

In this chapter, we introduce extreme sea kayaking, paint a watercolor portrait of the bold venture beyond the shore, and tell a little about ourselves and how we got involved in the sport. The following chapters are arranged in a progressive order. It's essential to absorb the first three chapters on equipment, preparation, and reading the sea before launching into the later chapters, which detail increasingly more complex and dangerous activities.

Here's a preview of the upcoming chapters. In chapter 2, "The Right Stuff," we look at the pros and cons of everything you'll need to wear and carry with you to brave the high seas. We recommend which types of kayak and paddle function best in the marine environment and offer our suggestions as to the most appropriate clothing and gear for safety and comfort. By heeding our advice in chapter 2, you'll save not only time and money but your hide as well.

Essential skills is the theme of chapter 3. We divide it into three sections: physical fitness and cross-training, psychological and mental fitness, and basic water and paddling skills. *Basic* skills, common to all extreme sea kayaking situations, include survival swimming, slalom paddle strokes, Eskimo rolling, and self-rescues. Upon completion of chapter 3, you can jump in your neighborhood pool and start practicing these essential skills to prepare yourself for the rigors of ocean whitewater.

Before venturing out, you need to know what you're getting into, so in chapter 4, "The Mighty Sea," we describe typical ocean features, conditions, and hazards, and how to read and navigate them. We compare and contrast reading the ocean with reading a river and introduce an ocean classifying system similar to the international system used to determine the difficulty and danger of a river section. After reading chapter 4, you'll be able to sit yourself down at a headland, read the wind and water, and visualize yourself in the picture.

Kayak surfing is the subject of chapter 5, "The Surf Zone." Surfing is an *intermediate* skill needed to handle storm seas and rock gardens. In this chapter, the ins and outs of the surf zone are detailed, along with surf etiquette, safety, and surfing tricks. Once you read our anecdotes and pore over our safety tips, you'll approach the surf with the

Metamorphosis of an Amphibian

I was raised in northern California, under the volcanic shadows of Mounts Shasta and Lassen. When I was two, my family took me camping at Hat Creek near Mount Lassen. The instant they turned their backs I was in the water, and someone had to run along the rapids and pluck me out of the snowmelt water. I thought it was great fun. But my dad thought he better teach me how to swim, so when I was five he would take me to the Redding Plunge and toss coins into the deep end of the pool. I quickly learned how to dive and swim underwater, as well as the value of money.

My family lived on a small ranch and raised a few head of cattle. As a youth, my job was irrigating the fields. In the summer, twice a week, I'd run a mile up to a canal, open the flume, and ride the tide of water back down to our land. In the heat of the day, I would run through the flooded fields and slide in the cool, cool water. By the time I was ten, my brother Marc and I swam all day, every day, during the summer—in pools, ponds, lakes, streams, canals, and rivers.

Then, one magic day, our dad took us to Ocean Beach in San Francisco. It was foggy, windy, and cold, and no one else was in the water, but we wanted to swim. He assured us that sharks didn't like the cold water (we learned later that 20-foot great white sharks did) and that the surf was safe. We raced the foam at the water's edge, challenged the breakers as they hit us in the chest, and went body-surfing until we were as cold as icicles. I returned to the mountains in love with the ocean. I dreamed about it, pictured myself inside ocean paintings, devoured books like Treasure Island, *and fantasized about becoming a navy frogman when I grew up.*

During our teens, Marc and I competed on swim teams, swam like otters in rushing mountain creeks, sailed in regattas, and paddled our family canoe. Early one spring we attempted to run the frothing upper Sacramento River at flood stage and wrapped our faithful Grumman around a rock, losing our camping gear. That was my first warning that water sports demanded lots more skill and judgment than I had imagined.

I joined the navy and spent two years before the mast in a man-o'-war, body-surfing exotic beach breaks around the Pacific. I abandoned the sea commando dream but learned scuba diving and explored the oceanic underworld.

Returning home, I ran into my high school friend Jim Kakuk, who had evolved into the kayak master of the nearby Burnt River Gorge. He gave me a slalom kayak, pointed to a whitewater rapid, and said, "Get in and go." I did and was immediately hooked on this high-adrenaline sport.

I taught myself the Eskimo roll in a frog pond before moving to Santa Barbara to attend college. Here there were no rivers but an ocean full of wonderful waves. Every afternoon after

(continued on page 8)

(continued from page 7)

class, I would race down to the beach near the university campus and surf until dark with my river kayak.

In 1983, I moved to the San Francisco Bay area, as did my old friend Jim Kakuk. Since he introduced me to river kayaking, I was delighted to return the favor and teach him how to surf kayak. I said, "Get in and go." He did and was soon hooked.

Jim and I began experimenting with different types of kayaks and gear. We finally mustered the courage to paddle out to north-facing Pedro Point at Pacifica, which was exposed to the big storm swells rolling down from the Gulf of Alaska. Its rocks and waves created a chaotic and dangerous environment, way beyond our skill level or understanding. But it inspired us to form a team to kayak and explore the unknown ocean environment. It was there that the idea of the Tsunami Rangers was born.

—Eric Soares

respect it deserves and will be acquainted with the rules of the road.

In chapter 6, we discuss how to paddle the open ocean in storm conditions and tour the exposed coast. You'll learn how to paddle when the seas are swept by powerful winds and how to launch and land kayaks in surf when touring. We describe the ideal exposed-coast campsite and provide instructive stories on open crossings and expeditions in faraway seas. When you finish chapter 6, you will know what to expect when you go *out there*, and you can then find a safe place to challenge the wind and to begin developing heavy weather skills.

Eric Soares goes airborne after punching through a wave at Rodeo Beach.

Jim Kakuk

How to place yourself in a rocky seascape painting is covered in chapter 7, "Ocean Rock Gardens." The features and dangers of ocean rock gardens are discussed in this chapter. *Advanced* techniques, such as positioning and seal landings, are described, along with how to avoid collisions and handle contact with rocks. Chapter 7 is a must-read for anyone contemplating a foray into the rocky minefields of the sea.

Paddling in sea caves is potentially the most extreme sea kayaking imaginable. In chapter 8, we showcase sea cave features and hazards. Tips for paddling in this dark, enclosed environment are provided, as are procedures for performing rescues. Our advice: don't be lured into a seemingly mellow sea cave. Read chapter 8 first!

In chapter 9, "Power of the Tribe," we advocate kayaking as a team to maximize safety and enjoyment. We compare groups with teams and explain team structure and function. We list hand signals that kayakers can use to communicate on the water. The ways in which experienced paddlers can guide newcomers through progressively more challenging conditions are carefully explained. After perusing chapter 9, you will be convinced of the power of the tribe.

No book on seafaring would be complete without sea stories. In chapter 10, "Out There," we provide a few more fables—and their morals. Oral history keeps the maritime traditions alive. Read these stories aloud; then go out and create your own legacy.

In chapter 11, "Resources," we identify some of our favorite books and other sources of information for the extreme sea kayaker.

We hope that *Extreme Sea Kayaking* will provide you with some enticing glimpses of the world of adventure

At the water's edge.

Jim Kakuk

that awaits beyond the shore, out on the outer edges of our water planet. Through the words and images gathered here, we share what we've learned from generations of intrepid and resourceful kayakers who preceded us into the sea. We encourage you to carry your boat to the water's edge and slip away into that world. If you are not already doing so, this book may inspire you to prepare yourself and venture out to sea by kayak. Then you will discover why paddling into a realm just as mysterious and humbling today as it was for those brave sea hunters centuries ago is deeply replenishing for the body and soul. For to go to sea in a lithesome, silent kayak is, in a very real way, to become wild and free again. We hope to encounter you soon, out there among the waves and the sky.

2 The Right Stuff

> "To be adventurous, you don't have to be the greatest or specially gifted. You just have to get inventive, get outfitted, then get out and try. There are great rewards."
> —Ned Gillette, mountaineer

To engage in extreme sea kayaking safely, as in mountaineering, do not compromise on equipment—the boat, paddle, clothing, and other gear upon which your comfort, and perhaps your very life, will depend. Let's look at the pros and cons of each, beginning with the most fundamental item, your boat.

Different Boats for Different Blokes

Modern sea kayaks are designed for efficiency and speed, with higher-end models incorporating exotic space-age materials for maximum strength and minimum weight. Long and sleek, they are beautiful and exciting to behold, slicing nimbly through the sea or accelerating down the face of a big wave. River kayak design, on the other hand, has gravitated toward shorter slalom-type boats, which are easy to maneuver in tight quarters. Both have been used for surf-zone ocean paddling, with varying degrees of success. Folks just learning to

kayak are often drawn to inexpensive, rotomolded plastic "sit-on-top" boats, which require little or no experience to paddle in calm water. However, the realm of extreme-condition sea kayaking demands a boat designed and built without compromise, and commitment to an extensive learning curve to acquire the skills necessary to operate it safely.

Ocean kayak surfing and rock garden exploration demand a tough, maneuverable boat. A short, plastic, rockered slalom boat like the closed-cockpit Perception Pirouette or the sit-on-top Ocean Kayak Yahoo is an inexpensive and reasonably satisfactory solution. Both boats sell for well under $1,000 new and can be found used for under $500 (1999 prices throughout). Plastic slalom boats such as these can take a beating and be used for many years as ocean whitewater play boats. If you are strapped for cash, get a used boat.

The Ideal Kayak for the Marine Environment

If you plan on engaging in multiday coastal exploration or other extended wilderness kayaking adventures, you need a boat designed for expedition paddling. Here you will be traveling longer distances and will need to carry a lot of food and camping gear. Yet you may also have to enter surf zones and other demanding and potentially dangerous conditions to land on and launch from remote beaches that face the open sea.

The rugged northern California coast, regularly battered by some of the biggest and most violent surf in the world, has provided a perfect environment in which to evolve expedition sea kayak design. The Tsunami Rangers, the Banzai Bozos, and Force Ten are three extreme-condition sea kayaking groups headquartered there. They have found specially designed and equipped sit-on-top, or "wash-deck," kayaks to be ideally suited to exposed-coast conditions. Since every boat has its strengths and weaknesses, it is a toss-up as to which particular kayak is the ideal boat. But there is one that might get the honors, the Tsunami X-15 Scramjet.

Tsunami Rangers Glenn Gilchrist and Jim Kakuk designed and Jim builds the Tsunami X-15, which they feel is the near-perfect kayak for exploring the marine environment. The Kevlar-armored X-15 is strong but lightweight, 14 feet long, and 24 inches wide, with moderate rocker so it can maneuver easily and a kick-up rudder with adjustable foot pedals for tracking. These hand-built boats are custom-made to order and cost $3,000.

Like all Tsunami boats, the X-15 features a sit-on-top cockpit with a quick-release seat belt that allows a skilled paddler to Eskimo roll, and large hatches with plenty of cargo space below for camping and diving gear and supplies. The boat weighs 50 pounds and can carry a big paddler and 100 pounds of gear. Because of its performance capabilities and versatility, the X-15 is the boat of choice for most of the Tsunami Rangers. (See chapter 11, "Resources," for a phone number for obtaining information about the X-15 and other Tsunami models.)

For extended coastal expeditions, the Rangers paddle the Tsunami X-2 Starship (cost is $4,000), a 20-foot wash-deck tandem kayak that is 26.5 inches wide at the beam and weighs 90 pounds. The X-2 (and its 24-foot cousin, the X-3) is similar to the X-15 except it holds two paddlers and a month's worth of gear. The Rangers also use the stable X-2 for rescues, photography, and diving.

The Mariner Coaster, similar to the X-15 in many respects, sans rudder and wash-deck cockpit, is Ranger John Lull's boat of choice and a model popular among many exposed-coast paddlers who prefer the snug feel of a closed cockpit and spray skirt. The Coaster is available from Mariner Kayaks for about $2,500.

A Tsunami X-15 Scramjet on the left and a Tsunami X-0 Crossover on the right.

Lower-end craft similar to the X-15 such as the Necky Dolphin, Prijon Twister, and the many Ocean Kayak models are mass-produced from rotomolded plastic. These boats are heavier and slower and lack the beauty and elegance of hand-crafted composite models, but they are much cheaper and very difficult to break.

Any Craft Will Do

In the hands of an expert, just about any sea kayak or decked canoe might be used for extreme sea kayaking. Even a handmade Hypalon-skinned baidarka (cost is around $800 for materials excluding labor) or inflatable Sevylor-type kayak will work adequately under certain conditions. Inflatable boats such as Aire's Lynx or Force IK (cost is $1,000) are used to run Class 3 rivers and have the advantage of portability, which makes them good for air travel. Regrettably, inflatable kayaks are very slow and susceptible to wind drag, which makes them poor choices for the exposed coast.

A long, touring sea kayak made of fiberglass (average cost is $2,200, with a 19-foot Eskimo 19 CRX Harpoon TR selling for $2,800) has the advantage of being extremely fast, but it could break from banging into rocks or even from wave compression when being pitch-poled in big surf. If you plan to paddle in surf zones and other extreme conditions, you can request a builder to custom-fabricate a composite kayak with an extra heavy layup of fiberglass or Kevlar on the hull bottom and other impact areas. This provides added strength but also increases the weight of the boat. The boat also becomes expensive (over $2,600, with the Eskimo 19 selling for $3,300 in a Kevlar-graphite composite). On the other hand, blow-molded plastic boats such as Prijon's popular Seayak, a 15-foot, 58-pound touring kayak, hold up well and cost only $1,100. The good news is that there are dozens of touring kayak manufacturers and hundreds of kayak shops all over the United States with models for testing.

Again, rotomolded plastic sit-on-top models, such as the Dagger Cayman and Ocean Kayak Scrambler, are inexpensive (under $1,000), durable options for the entry-level or casual paddler who wants to try a little surfing and rock bashing. These big manufacturers have popularized the use of these wide, stable, sit-on-top kayaks that require little skill or experience to operate. Yet, the width and volume that give these boats stability also make them slow and cumbersome to handle in pushy wind and water. Most of these boats come equipped only with thigh braces, not seat belts, so there's always the likelihood of becoming suddenly separated from one's boat in breaking surf. For these reasons, few expert paddlers consider these models adequate for true extreme-condition paddling.

Wooden kayaks, like those offered in kit form by Pygmy Kayaks (kit cost is $500 and up), are light, responsive to paddle, and quite beautiful. But most aficionados

who have painstakingly crafted one by hand would never dream of taking it anywhere near surf and rocks. In the final analysis, wooden boats are too delicate for serious rock bashing.

Folding boats (e.g., Klepper, Folbot, Feathercraft) have the advantage of being easy to transport by bush plane or public transportation to remote locations, but they are slow and generally too fragile to withstand contact with rocks or barnacles or to hold up to other rigors of extreme-condition sea kayaking. In addition, they are very expensive (a Feathercraft K1 Expedition sold for $3,780).

Sit-on-top surf skis like the Futura, Valhalla, and Twogood are popular for open-water races like across the Molokai Channel but are too tippy and fragile for surf zones and rock gardens. The 18-foot Futura II cost $1,500 in 1998 for a standard fiberglass layup. The Odyssea Surf Ski (cost is about $2,500), paddled by Force Ten, is a heavily reinforced fiberglass ski with hatches for storing gear and is suitable for extreme sea kayaking, especially storm kayaking.

Sit-on-Top versus Closed-Cockpit Boats

A basic decision every kayaker faces is whether to paddle a skirted (closed-cockpit) or a sit-on-top (wash-deck) boat. A closed-cockpit kayak will keep you drier and more protected from the elements, until you capsize. Your lower torso is inside of, rather than on top of, the craft, and this can bring a greater feeling of *connectedness* with your boat. Closed-cockpit boats allow your legs to sit lower and provide more support for your lower back, which may be more comfortable for some people in the long haul.

The main disadvantage of a closed-cockpit boat is a significant consideration in extreme-condition paddling. When you capsize with a closed cockpit and fail to Eskimo roll, you are then forced to come out of the boat (make a wet exit). Self-rescue then becomes problematic. However, in a wash-deck boat, you sit *on* it, not *in* a cockpit with a spray skirt. When you capsize with a sit-on-top, all you have to do is clamber back on—the boat does not fill up with wa-

Jim Kakuk

Sit-on-top versus closed-cockpit slalom kayaks.

Eric Soares tests a Tsunami X-7 Mojo prototype.

roughest water. Remember that quick-release seat belts require the user to actively disengage them, just as closed-cockpit paddlers must actively pull the skirt off and squirm out of their boats. There is a danger of entrapment in either a closed- or open-cockpit kayak, should a paddler panic or become disabled while capsized and fail to release the seat belt or remove the skirt. Before setting out, always practice disengaging your seat belt or skirt with your eyes closed to be sure you can accomplish this lifesaving move smoothly when you find yourself upside down and underwater.

The only sure way to determine what is the best extreme-condition kayak for you is to get out and paddle as many different models as possible in challenging conditions. It's unlikely you will get much of a sense of a performance boat's real capabilities (and limitations) in flat water. When putting a new boat through its paces, be aware of how it *feels* to your body and how it responds to your particular paddling style. Note that every boat has its strengths and weaknesses, so choose a boat that you believe is best for you. Also, note that new models are being designed all the time, just as older models are no longer

ter as does a closed-cockpit boat. If you've managed to hold onto your paddle, you're immediately ready for action again.

Seat belts are employed on some high-performance sit-on-top kayaks such as the Tsunami X-15 and Odyssea Surf Ski to enable a paddler to remain seated in the craft and perform leaning braces and Eskimo rolls, even in the

being built. Sea kayaking symposia and watersport dealers' demo days are good opportunities to test a variety of makes and models.

Rudder or Not

Rudders represent another choice. The original native kayakers never employed rudders on their baidarkas. Highly rockered river and slalom boats have no use for rudders when used for their original purposes, but some paddlers have added fins or skegs to them for ocean surfing. Many modern sea kayaks, including most of the Tsunami boats, employ rudders. They make steering and tracking with a longer boat easier, especially when strong winds and currents are present.

Unfortunately, being the only moving parts of a kayak, rudders can jam and break unexpectedly. If you are venturing far, it's wise to include a spare rudder blade, cables, and the tools necessary to fix anything that breaks. Eric, on an expedition down the remote Lost Coast of northern California, broke six rudders in seven days of launching and landing his heavily laden X-2 through big surf on steep, cobbled beaches.

Rudder systems add $100 or more to the cost of a boat. Tsunami Products fabricates Kevlar rudder blades that sell for $35 each.

Up a Creek with a Paddle

A paddle is your direct physical connection with the sea that surrounds you, and selecting the right one is as important as your choice of boat. For extreme sea kayaking, a paddle should be light, strong, slightly flexible, and able to transmit your every impulse to the water energetically and efficiently. Traditional Aleut and Inuit paddles were made from a variety of gathered materials and generally had relatively long, slender blades. This beautiful style of blade, while still popular for touring, lacks the power and control necessary for intense surf zone and ocean whitewater activity.

Wing paddles, developed by Stephan Lindeberg of Sweden for flatwater racing, are also inappropriate for extreme-condition kayaking because their radical shape makes bracing, ruddering, and rolling difficult. They are also too fragile to survive long in surf and around rocks. Wide-bladed, slalom river kayaking paddles, designed for strength, maneuverability, and delivering intense bursts of power, work best.

Modern paddles are fashioned of laminated wood, fiberglass, and exotic composites like carbon fiber and Kevlar. There are even paddle makers who make custom models for customers. The Tsunami Rangers continue to experiment with different brands and materials. Michael Powers prefers the warm, natural feel of wood and uses a hand-crafted whitewater model made by Sawyer ($200). Eric Soares and Jim Kakuk favor a flat-bladed surf paddle ($150) designed by Merv Larson and made of a Kevlar-graphite composite by Tsunami. Extreme sea kayaking often involves venturing into exposed areas where winds are strong. A feathered paddle, with one blade offset 60 to 90 degrees from the other, reduces the surface area of the up-raised blade exposed to headwinds.

You'll be holding your paddle hour after hour, day after day, so make sure it is comfortable, lightweight, and tough. Also, for expeditions, each kayaker should bring a spare break-apart paddle, just in case. We sometimes bring T-handles (canoe handles) to place inside break-apart shafts to make canoe paddles, which are just the right size for narrow confines in caves.

What Shall I Wear?

The clothes protecting your body are your final line of defense in extreme sea kayaking and can make the difference between life and death. The cold hard fact is that the majority of sea kayaking tragedies and traumas are caused by hypothermia, produced in part by wearing clothing inappropriate for the water temperature and conditions. A capsize in cold water is sure to convince you that proper clothing is a worthwhile investment.

Watersport clothing must fulfill two important functions: it must keep you warm and must protect your body from impact and abrasion with unfriendly obstacles, such as other boats and rocks. Since getting cold is a major contributing factor in so many sea kayaking fatalities, the importance of dressing for the water temperature (not the air temperature) cannot be overemphasized. Immersion in water is an inevitable side effect of extreme sea kayaking. Always dress for extreme-condition kayaking in a manner that will allow you to survive comfortably in cold water for extended periods.

Nani Venegas is ready to face the surf zone.

The Inside Scoop on Underclothing

Stretchable fabric liners underneath wet- and drysuits have become popular in recent years. They provide added warmth, reduce chafing, and can make pulling a wetsuit on and off a lot easier. For centuries, the

Broken Boat, Broken Paddle

One day a squad of Tsunami Ranger officers and cadets were on an exploratory mission near Pigeon Point, on the northern California coast. The seas got rough, so Captain Jim Kakuk ordered everyone to head toward shore, with me designated as sweep. After everyone else had reached the safety of a cove, I lingered to surf the refracting waves offshore. Suddenly, a rogue wave 15 feet high came roaring around the point, and I knew I was caught inside with no escape route. Realizing I was going to get hit hard, I relaxed everything except my grip on the paddle and breathed deeply and slowly. Then the big wave slammed down on me.

After the initial impact, I felt myself being dragged and bounced across the rocky reef, directly toward the cliff. I threw my whole weight into the wave and dug in, knowing that was my only chance to remain upright. I felt my paddle banging across the reef. Even with its reinforced tip and heavy-duty, Kevlar-armored layup, I knew it couldn't take this abuse for long, and suddenly I heard the extended blade crack and break off. I looked at my hand scraping along just inches above the rocks and prayed my paddle shaft would hold up for just a few seconds longer. It did.

I was swept down 8 feet onto a lower shelf next to the cliff and felt tons of water cascade down upon me. I heard a crackling peal as the hull and deck shuddered under the impact. Light and energy seemed to radiate around me during those long moments. I swear I heard angels gibbering around my head. Then the wave receded, and all was suddenly calm. My beautiful Tsunami X-1 was cracked in several places and was filling with water. Miraculously, the boat and paddle had shielded me from the repeated impact, and I was not injured. I swam with my boat and paddle into safer water. My companions, who had watched helplessly from inside the reef, could now approach and tow my boat, while I swam the remaining 200 meters to the beach. Once we reached shore, I jumped for joy. It felt wonderful to be alive!

Lessons learned: First of all, I exercised bad judgment by approaching an unfamiliar reef in such big seas without first scouting it thoroughly. Next, I was reminded that in extreme conditions, even the hardiest equipment can break, reinforcing our policy of always seeking out the toughest gear available. In many instances, gear has made a crucial difference. Also, the time-tested maxim of keeping the boat between one's body and the rocks, allowing it and not our bodies to take the beating, paid off once more. Another principle that again proved its importance was our policy to never go into extreme situations alone. Having other skilled team members nearby with tow ropes probably saved what was left of my boat in this situation. And finally, just remaining relaxed, even in what appeared to be a hopeless situation, undoubtedly contributed to my not being injured. Relax, go with the flow, but never give up.

—Eric

Scandinavians and other northern peoples have relied upon wool for survival on blustery seas, but most Americans consider it too scratchy to wear next to their skin. Cotton dries slowly, is a poor insulator when wet, and is unsatisfactory for watersports. Nylon underclothing is relatively inexpensive and good for chafing protection, but it is not warm. Polypropylene underclothing is very warm for its weight and shares with nylon the advantage of drying quickly. Generic polypropylene shirts cost less than $50 today. The downside is the material tends to retain odors, as anyone who has ever driven home from a long sea kayaking trip with a pile of damp polypro in the back of the car can testify.

Some paddlers wear TiCoat, Thermalastic, and Thermal Stretch bodysuits, hybrids between neoprene wetsuits and nylon tights. They provide warmth and protection from abrasion but are very expensive today ($200 for a bodysuit).

Wetsuits versus Drysuits

Thanks to innovative watersport clothing manufacturers like O'Neill, MTI, Kokatat, Patagonia, and Stohlquist, many options are now available to the cold-water paddler. Some extreme-condition kayakers, including the majority of the Tsunami Rangers, prefer full-body, one-piece, neoprene wetsuits for paddling in cold (lower than 60°F) water. Wetsuits designed for diving are too restrictive for the repetitive shoulder and arm movements of paddling, so get wetsuits custom-made with gussets under the armpits, body-contoured torsos, and extra neoprene for the butt and legs. A custom wetsuit costs about $300 from Heat Wave in Santa Cruz—and it's worth it.

Some extreme sea kayakers prefer the modular wetsuit approach, which offers the greatest flexibility as conditions change. The modular suit begins with a 3- to 5-mm-thick farmer john with optional padded knees. Over that, you can wear a 5-mm wetsuit top with 3-mm arms and a connected 3- to 5-mm hood with built-in sun visor.

If you are of average build and want to save $100 on your wetsuit, you may find off-the-rack surfer's wetsuits fit well enough. But check any suit you are considering to ensure it allows a full range of upper torso movement with no "bungee cord" effect, especially through the shoulders.

Jim Kakuk

A custom-made wetsuit is the most comfortable choice.

For 50°F water, the ideal paddling suit should have a 5-mm-thick neoprene body with 3-mm-thick shoulders and arms and gussets under the armpits to allow full freedom of motion for the shoulders. Eric prefers a suit with kneepads and extra latex extending past the wrists so he can roll it down over his gloves or roll it back to keep his wrists warm. The main zipper should be in the back and should be insulated with a neoprene flap. The neck of a suit must not be so tight as to restrict breathing or cause chafing. Zippers on a suit's ankles make it easier to pull on and off when you are cold and tired.

A medium to heavyweight nylon, wool, or polypro fleece paddling sweater ($70) worn in combination with a sleeveless farmer john neoprene wetsuit ($100) and underneath a waterproof nylon paddling jacket ($100) or drysuit top ($150) provides the most freedom of movement for the arms and shoulders. A potential disadvantage of paddling jackets in extreme conditions is that the sleeves fill up with water when a paddler is swimming. When the water is cold, you may wish to add a neoprene tank top vest with a built-in hood ($60) worn under the wetsuit or paddling jacket to provide warmth to your head and prevent water from rushing down your neck.

If you paddle in tropical conditions where both the water and air temperatures are warm (72°F or above), a Thermalastic suit or 2-mm-thick neoprene shortie wetsuit may provide adequate warmth and protection. But in temperate and subarctic climates, it is common during the summer months for the air temperature to be warm while the water remains cold. In such circumstances, light clothing, or even a heavier weight farmer john worn by itself, is inadequate. In the event of capsize, water will gush in through the arm and neck openings, chilling and incapacitating the unfortunate kayaker who is forced to remain in the cold water very long.

The bottom line: it is always better to be overprotected than underprotected. A warmly dressed paddler can always slip off a layer of clothing, do an Eskimo roll, or slip off a wash-deck boat to cool down.

For frigid air and water conditions (40°F and below), a kayaker's (not a diver's) drysuit, in combination with polypropylene underwear and layers of fleece underclothing, provides the ultimate thermal protection. A Kokatat, NRS, or Stohlquist full drysuit costs between $350 and $500. However, drysuits have one serious drawback that limits their usefulness for extreme sea kayaking: if they become torn, they can fill up quickly with water. Don't wear them if you plan on paddling through rock gardens and sea caves. Other problems with drysuits are overheating and the difficulty of relieving oneself without going ashore.

A Reef Tiger Attacked My Drysuit

One blustery January day, we were kayaking along the northern California coast a few miles south of San Francisco. Approaching a partially exposed reef system about 1,000 feet offshore, we waited for a lull in the big surf and then charged in to accomplish a seal landing on a low-lying islet known as Flat Rock. Eric reentered the surf zone in his X-1 Rocket Boat, while Michael clambered 100 feet seaward along the reef to film him with a movie camera. Since waves were periodically breaking over the reef, Jim Kakuk remained with the boats. He was wearing a brand-new drysuit that a manufacturer had given the Rangers to try out. Jim was impressed with the freedom of movement and how warm it kept him, in spite of the winter storm bearing down upon the Pacific coast at the time.

A big set of waves moved in, each more powerful than the last. Then a huge wave arrived, and Michael glanced up from where he was barely maintaining his own footing to see Jim and their two kayaks swept off Flat Rock and into the tumultuous sea. At first this seemed funny, until it became apparent that Jim was in trouble. Eric paddled over to Jim to find him struggling to reenter his boat. The seat of Jim's new drysuit had become shredded by his passage across the jagged reef, and the suit had filled with water. It looked like a tiger had taken a swipe at his backside. Eric helped him get back on his boat and then pushed Michael's boat back to the reef.

Jim was scraped and bruised during his tumble over the rocks because, unlike a thick neoprene wetsuit, the drysuit had no significant padding. Jim found that swimming in the swamped suit was nearly impossible, and he got cold quickly. Based on this and other experiences, the Tsunami Rangers have concluded that drysuits, surf, and rocks are a dangerous combination.

Hoods and Hats

Choice of headgear is highly personal, and paddlers can be found wearing knitted wool and fleece caps, New England sailor's hats, balaclavas, visored caps, and even ornate replicas of traditional Aleut hunting hats. All these have their place in the realm of sea kayak touring under ordinary circumstances. However, paddling in storm surf, subarctic climates, and other extreme conditions where exposure or immersion would soon prove fatal to the unprotected human body demands time-tested, expedition-quality apparel.

Hoods and skull caps help keep water out of the ears and provide critical abrasion and thermal protection to the neck and head, parts of the body that lose a tremendous amount of body heat when exposed to the elements. A diving hood ($25 to $40) that extends down the neck to overlap the wetsuit will prevent icy water from rushing down the neck. Wool, Polyfleece, or Thermalastic caps may be adequate in moderate conditions, but if the water is 50°F or colder, a neoprene hood or hat becomes a critically important part of one's protective apparel. Thermal Stretch scull caps ($20) are a handy item to carry along, as a first line of defense or to wear under hoods for extra warmth.

For protection from the sun's burning rays, a wide-brimmed hat or cap or a hood with a visor works well. Neoprene visors ($20) are good in the surf zone because they flex under pressure. In warmer climates, a breathable fabric hat or visored cloth cap that can be worn under your helmet is fairly comfortable.

Helmets

Any time you paddle near surf and rocks, head protection is *absolutely essential*. It's imperative that you wear a helmet specially designed and built for watersports—headgear made for other activities may not be satisfactory for kayaking for a number of reasons. Most motorcycle and football helmets are too heavy and may be constructed of materials that absorb water. Climbing helmets are designed primarily to take the impact of rocks falling from above, an unlikely scenario for paddlers. Ice hockey helmets may work fairly well at first, but the hardware can corrode quickly in salt water. Shun those stylish river rodeo helmets with odd angles sticking out if you will be facing heavy ocean hydraulics. They can act like scoops for water under pressure, placing sudden strain on the wearer's neck and possibly causing the helmet to be torn off, just when needed most.

The best headgear for extreme sea kayaking is a lightweight, high-impact plastic or Kevlar-shelled helmet, designed specifically for watersports. These can be padded

either by a web arrangement or with closed-cell foam and should feature a sturdy, quick-release buckle.

Romer, Pro-tec, Primex, Prijon, Bell, and Cascade all make helmets specifically for watersports at prices starting at $50. On the other hand, the Prijon Korsika helmet with extended face guard costs $135. Gath offers a lightweight helmet that has become popular with board surfers, with an optional, retractable, tinted, see-through Lexan shield that protects the face from oncoming waves for about $140. For $20 less, Deluge offers a helmet with an optional, vinyl-coated steel screen, similar to a hockey or football cage.

Misha Dynnikov

Michael Powers had his helmet torn off his head by powerful hydraulics.

If you plan to venture near rocks and into sea caves often, face protection might be a good idea. The jury is still out on this because it is possible that extreme impact might break the screen and force it back into the face and eyes. Also, it's harder to see with all that extra stuff hanging in front of your face. The main thing is that you test helmets, select one, and always wear it in extreme-condition paddling.

Footwear

Neoprene, polypropylene, Thermal Stretch, and wool all continue to provide thermal protection when wet, which makes them useful for watersports sock material. Polypro has the added advantage of drying quickly. When the water is cold,

below 50°F, a pair of these socks worn inside your neoprene booties makes them much warmer.

Thick, nonslip soles are crucial to safely clambering over wet rocks, and neoprene divers' booties with substantial soles allow you to dig in when carrying boats and gear down a steep hillside to the sea and protect you from sea urchin spicules. Zippers on booties make them easier to get on and off, but the downside is that even a few grains of sand can jam them. All Tsunami Rangers wear divers' booties when we kayak on the exposed coast.

the money if you expect to do much swimming in surf zones or climbing on slippery rocks and cliffs. NRS ATB Wetshoes ($55) are an inexpensive alternative that also function well in the marine environment. Cheap neoprene reef shoes found in drugstores for $10 work about as well, though they don't last very long.

In cold, wet climates like Alaska and Tierra del Fuego, fishermen's rubber boots and thick socks are the footwear combination of choice when sea kayak touring. No doubt, warm, dry feet are wonderful when kayaking in

High-end footwear (about $100) designed specifically for demanding aquatic activities, like the Okéspor and the Patagonia CFS (cubic feet per second), combine the best features of climbing and watersports shoes. They feature thick, nonslip soles and sophisticated closure systems, usually combinations of lacing and Velcro, to ensure they can't be ripped off in the intense hydraulics of a whitewater river or ocean surf zone. They are costly but worth

cold weather, but when you capsize, rubber boots will immediately fill with water, making swimming extremely difficult. These should *never* be worn while kayaking but are great around cold, soggy camps.

River sandals work fine in climates like Baja and Hawaii, although the protection they provide from sting

> **Helmets with face guards provide additional face protection when worn in extreme conditions.**

rays, thorns, and other nasties is minimal. Remember, it's a jungle out there, and going nearly barefoot can be tough on unprotected feet.

Gloves

Neoprene, thin enough (1 to 2 mm) so as not to interfere with your grip on the paddle, is the usual choice of material for kayaking in medium to moderately cold water. Sailing gloves, which come in both fingerless and full-fingered models, are lightweight neoprene on top and thin leather on the inner palm surfaces to afford some protection, while retaining most of the dexterity of bare hands and their feel for the paddle shaft. Neoprene gloves are now being made with the fingers precurved to make gripping a paddle easier, all for about $20 to $30. Other than that, there are fishing gloves (cheap), football receiver gloves (expensive), and bicycling gloves (the padded palms interfere with your feel of the paddle shaft). Gloves made for diving are generally too thick and inflexible for gripping a paddle comfortably for long lengths of time and make dexterity tasks difficult. An inexpensive and easily obtainable alternative is ordinary dishwashing gloves, which protect surprisingly well against abrasion, wind, and sunburn and cost less than $5.

In extreme cold and wind, however, even thick wet neoprene can seem to wick heat away from continually exposed hands. One solution to this problem is pogies (about $30), an outer shell of water-resistant fabric that slips over the gloved hand and then snaps or fastens with Velcro around the paddle shaft. These work all right if you are content to have your hands attached continuously to the paddle shaft. But photographers or anyone who needs to have their hands free, such as extreme sea kayakers, will find them frustrating. Paddling in subarctic northern Norway and Kodiak Island, the authors found the warmest gloves are those that actually keep the hands dry. In a diving shop we discovered the ultimate solution for extreme cold weather—$50 gloves made of rubber with Polyfleece liners and latex gaskets at the sleeves like the ones on drysuits.

Personal Flotation Devices

Coast Guard regulations require that every paddler have an approved personal flotation device (PFD) at the ready. Watersports associations, magazines, guidebooks, outfitters, and retailers concur that a life vest is absolutely essential to safety on the water. Unquestionably, PFDs save many lives each year. Yet it's foolhardy to think that wearing such a device makes one safe on the water. There are hazardous circumstances where merely remaining on the surface isn't enough to ensure survival—powerful hydraulics and currents that can sweep a swimmer far away from shore, breaking waves that can hurtle an out-of-control paddler over jagged rocks, cold water that can induce hypothermia.

There are some iconoclasts among the extreme sea kayaking community who question the edict that a PFD should be worn by all paddlers in all circumstances. Eric, for example, believes that wearing a PFD is a personal choice. His reasoning is that ocean distance swimmers don't wear them, surfers don't wear them, divers don't wear them, seals don't wear them, so why should he have to just because he happens to be associated with a boat? Eric has found that a PFD, especially one with more than 20 pounds of flotation, interferes with some survival tactics, like diving underneath oncoming waves when capsized, swimming in surf zones and rock gardens, and even climbing back on or in your boat. Of course, he adds, if you consciously choose not to wear your PFD, you must be an excellent rough-water swimmer. Also, to avoid running afoul of the law, you still must have a PFD readily accessible on your vessel.

There are times when Eric dons his Lotus Rio Grande Type III PFD (with a little over 15 pounds of flotation and selling for $87). He wears it during open crossings to rest in the water while awaiting rescue, in storms and heavy wind for extra warmth, and around sharp rocks and flying boats to protect him from abrasion or sudden impact. Eric and fellow Ranger John Lull use the Lotus PFD because it zips up front (which makes it easy to get on and off), is simple and practical, tends not to ride up, and features pockets for stowing small items and for easy rescue.

For expeditions and extended coastal explorations by sea kayak, a PFD must perform other functions besides just providing buoyancy to its wearer. Michael uses the Discovery by MTI ($80) and finds it to be an excellent expedition vest. It features two large, self-draining pockets, two D-rings where a whistle, flares, and other emergency gear may be attached, a diving knife patch, a quick-release waist closure system, and reflective tape across the front and back for night visibility.

Before entrusting your life to a PFD, test it by swimming in heavy surf. Does it ride up and cover your face, or does it stay in position around your chest? Is it comfortable, and does it allow a full range of arm movement for swimming as well as paddling? One PFD that has become popular among extreme sea kayakers is the form-fitting, slipover squirt style, originally designed for acrobatic river paddlers. The flotation material is thick and concentrated across the chest and back in these vests, providing maximum protection in the event of a collision with another boat.

PFDs are evolving and getting better all the time. Huge, unmanageable kapok vests are rarely sold by dealers today, whereas space-age PFDs such as the comfortable and cool-looking Leonardo and Mona Lisa PFDs from Extrasport (about $150), made with state-of-the-art thermo-molded, bonded Airex foam, are on the rise. We have experimented with a variety of PFDs and other flotation systems, including divers' buoyancy compensators, which provide variable buoyancy but are expensive (over $200), complicated, not Coast Guard approved, and of limited use for extreme sea kayaking.

Remember, PFDs are not a panacea that will guarantee your safety on the water. Don't expect a life vest to always keep your head above the surface in rough water, especially if you are unconscious, paralyzed, or too numb with cold to tread water. Like wetsuits and helmets, they are a tool, effective in extreme conditions only when used properly in combination with skill and good judgment. Proper water clothing, strong swimming skills, and good physical condition are all at least as important as wearing a PFD in most extreme sea kayaking situations.

Flotsam and Jetsam

We've covered the essential gear you must have with you each time you venture away from shore to face extreme conditions in a sea kayak. Now let's consider some optional items you might wish to have along, depending on the nature, length, remoteness, and anticipated degree of risk on your sea journey.

Safety Gear

Safety and emergency gear takes up space in a kayak and adds weight—until there is a real emergency, when it suddenly becomes urgently needed. But what's reasonable? A doctor might stress medical equipment, whereas a climber would be expected to emphasize jumars, ropes, and a harness. A marine radio, EPIRB (emergency position-indicating radio beacon), and GPS (global positioning system) might be high on a bluewater sailor's list of priorities.

The nature of the trip will determine the appropriate safety gear. For example, on a sea kayaking and filmmaking expedition among the arctic Spitsbergen Islands, 900 miles north of continental Norway, Michael had to carry a high-powered rifle as well as trip wires set up around camp every night to trigger an explosive charge to warn if a polar bear approached. The presence of dangerous animals (two people had been killed by polar bears in recent months on Spitsbergen) demanded precautions that would be totally inappropriate on a sea kayaking trip along the coast of Big Sur. It's important to carefully weigh all factors, such as extremes of climate, remoteness of location, and exceptional health hazards, when selecting safety equipment for a sea kayaking journey.

Typically, our kayaking team will paddle a remote and unfamiliar stretch of coastline until a beach is discovered, preferably on an island or surrounded by high cliffs where human intrusion is unlikely. There we establish a base camp and stash our food, camping equipment, extra clothing, and water. This enables us to venture out on day trips with unladen, responsive boats to explore the area.

For paddling among rock gardens, surf and intertidal zones, and sea caves, each Ranger is expected to carry polypropylene or Spectra line and a throw bag with floating line and a stainless steel carabiner or two that may be quickly rigged for rescues or towing. Manufacturers such as NRS, Salamander, and Pro Guardian design good rescue bags that sell from $32 to $80. An old water-skier's belt with a floating line and D-rings attached makes an adequate rescue device to hand to panicked swimmers.

A small first-aid kit is always stashed away in each person's boat, as well as a roll of duct tape and a multitool ($10 to $100). Flotation bags, stuffed into the fore and aft hatches, are a must to ensure that even a badly damaged boat will remain buoyant. Bilge pumps, sponges, cameras, a water bottle, lunch, and a few energy bars complete the basic list of stuff carried for day paddling.

When the Rangers are on an extended expedition, especially if far from civilization (e.g., the southern tip of South America or the British Columbia archipelago), we carry a more extensive first-aid kit, such as the comprehensive Adventure Medical Kit ($142) designed by wilderness physician Eric Weiss. We bring along a portable VHF marine radio (about $300) to communicate with the Coast Guard and receive weather information. Each paddler also carries a waterproof signal kit ($20 to $50) on his person, such as the Skyblazer Marine Signal Pack, which contains aerial flares, a whistle, and a locator flag. To paddle at night or in dark sea caves, we also bring reflective tape, chemical light sticks to attach to the back of our helmets, and water-resistant headlamps such as the NiteRider Digital Explorer ($180).

Damage Control

Stainless steel multitools and Swiss Army knives are indispensable for accomplishing a multitude of tasks relating to sea kayak maintenance in the field. Major equipment damage, although common when paddling in extreme conditions, can usually be patched up temporarily with duct tape. Yet, on a multiday trip, it's a good idea to bring along a fiberglass repair kit, spare rudders, rudder cable, 100 feet of nylon line, 10 yards or so of bungee cord for deck lashing, and plenty of duct tape. It's surprising how many successful repairs have been accomplished in the field using duct tape, sometimes in combination with found materials.

Personal Gear

Sunscreen, sunglasses with retainers to prevent their getting lost, drinking water, and an energy bar in a waterproof wrapper are handy items to keep stashed in a small dry bag within easy reach when paddling. Another slightly larger dry bag will carry your lunch, a camera and extra film, and dry clothes (polypro balaclava and shirt, wool sweater, pile pants, and a waterproof shell) to change into when you leave the water and get cold. Also, an extra diving hood and neoprene vest can save the day if you are lightly dressed and a squall rolls in, causing the air temperature to plummet and a cold wind to rise. Fins, mask, and snorkel may come in handy, along with a spear gun or fishing gear. The fins should be kept handy to assist a swim-rescuer in turbulent water. Eric sometimes wears surf rescue fins made by Hydro ($70) while kayaking. The fins are small and lightweight.

Electronic Gizmos and Other Optional Gear

Because the essential gear you need costs a lot, think twice before dragging along expensive, complex gear you don't really need. For example, a hiker's compass, diver's wrist compass, or deck compass ($10 to $100) is useful for coastal navigation, especially in fog or at night. But do you really need an electronic GPS finder that costs at least $100 just to figure out where you are and where you are going? Do you *need* to have a handheld, waterproof, unsinkable, electronic anemometer that costs at least $100 to tell you the wind speed? Do you *need* an armored, electronic, waterproof wristwatch with built-in altimeter and barometer that costs at least $100 just to know that you are indeed at sea level and that it might rain?

Wave Warrior Armor

In the early 1980s, we began experimenting with athletic pads and body armor designed for other water- and land-based sports. To decrease injuries to the vulnerable chest and shoulders, we utilized motocross upper-body armor, martial arts and catcher's face guards, knee and shin pads, and hockey shoulder and elbow pads. While they lasted, these accessories did provide some protection and contributed to the Rangers' "wave warrior" image in the media. However, this stuff added weight, tended to snag on things, and frequently got torn off or shifted out of position by the intense hydraulics of the surf zone. Except when performing special stunts, we now usually wear just wetsuits, PFDs, and helmets for protection. We hope that lightweight body armor will be developed someday that replaces the PFD.

In summary, the list of items presented in this chapter is not exhaustive, and new products appear in the marketplace daily. Shop around, pester the experts, and try items out whenever possible before committing. The product reviews and buyer's guide sections of *Sea Kayaker*, *Paddler*, and *Canoe & Kayak* magazines are cornucopias of useful information (see chapter 11, "Resources").

Remember that even the best equipment will never replace good judgment and paddling skill for safety on the water. Still, having the right stuff with you out there can instill confidence and contribute immeasurably to your fun, comfort, and safety while paddling.

A team outfitted in full body armor, ready for a battle in the rocks.

Essential Skills

> ❝ Kayaking's not an *on*-water sport; it's an *in*-water sport! ❞
>
> —Steve Sinclair, storm sea kayaker

Being reasonably robust and athletic, in mind as well as body, is a distinct advantage for anyone entering the domain of the mighty sea in a tiny boat. However, it is imperative to be in good physical and mental condition to safely engage in extreme-condition ocean kayaking. This doesn't mean you must train like Greg Barton for the Olympic kayak races. But it's *crucial* that you possess good mind and body fitness and are a strong swimmer. Basic and intermediate paddling and self-rescue techniques are also prerequisites of extreme sea kayaking.

Because the sport is so demanding, and conditions are so wild and chaotic,

attention to the basics is called for in this chapter. We first look at the essential physical and mental preparation and skills needed for extreme sea kayaking. Then we focus on survival swimming techniques because this is an *in*-water sport. Finally, we discuss paddling strokes and self-rescues.

Physical Preparation —Shaping Up to Meet the Sea

A good starting point is an honest assessment of your physical condition as well as your in-the-water capabilities. Are you generally able to remain calm and in control when paddling in breaking waves or a powerful rip current? When was the last time you swam in a surf zone? Can you run a mile down the beach without becoming exhausted? The old "use it or lose it" edict applies here, and unless these survival and conditioning skills are practiced regularly, we can never be certain they will be there when we need them.

Strong swimming skills are a must.

Jim Kakuk

Physical Training

Like just about everything else in life, being in good shape helps us get the most out of ocean adventure kayaking. Yet, maintaining a high level of physical conditioning takes some conscious effort, especially as we get older. Sadly, there are many today whose busy indoor lifestyles have reduced the opportunity for outdoor physical activities. We've seen these folks sign up for adventure travel trips and fly off to exotic locales in hope of getting back in shape. All too frequently, enjoyment of their expensive vacations is diminished by injury, illness, or exhaustion. In particular, a multiday trek or sea kayaking expedition demands that we exert ourselves, sometimes strenuously and under demanding conditions, for extended periods without breaking down. *Now is the time to begin working to maintain (or regain) our strength and health, long before we embark upon that epic paddling adventure.*

Still, a word of caution is in order. A sudden leap from indolence into a strenuous training regime is never wise, and overtraining can be as harmful as doing nothing at all. In the beginning, one should exercise regularly but gently, allowing the body (and mind) time to adjust and grow stronger. Some form of activity every day is preferable to bingeing on weekends or vacations. Get a physical exam before engaging in any demanding and potentially dangerous sport, especially if you've been inactive for a while. If you suffer from seizures, cardiovascular problems, shoulder dislocation, or a bad back, extreme-condition sea kayaking may not be for you.

We have found that varying our exercise programs and engaging in cross-training help keep the body and mind flexible and resilient. The table above shows our physical training regimens, some part of which we do every day.

Notice that neither of us kayaks daily, even though we both live right next to the ocean and have the opportunity.

We have three reasons for this. First, we don't want to tire of the sport by doing it so often it becomes a job. Eric was a competition swimmer for six years when he was young; he got burned out from the monotonous chore of swimming lap after lap, year after year, and now will swim only for pleasure, not distance or time.

The second reason we don't kayak every day is we believe in the merits of a varied exercise palette. Though not sports physiology experts, we think cross-training is the way to go. It is more fun and better for the body. Eric does jujitsu 14 hours a week and finds it complements extreme

Michael	Eric
weight training in gym, 3x week run on the beach, 2x week attend yoga class, 2x week, + daily stretching outdoors building and gardening, as often as possible swim or kayak, 2–3x week	attend jujitsu class, 4x week play hacky sack, 3x week climb hills, 4x week stretch & do calisthenics, daily swim or kayak, weekly

sea kayaking, as does hacky sack, because all three activities require the body and mind to react quickly and accurately to stimuli. Yet, each is unique and fun in its own way.

Avoiding injury is the third reason we cross-train instead of concentrating all our physical exertion on kayaking. We don't want to suffer repetitive motion injuries from doing the same activity over and over.

Avoiding Injuries

A benefit of being in great shape is the reduction in strains, sprains, dislocations, and even broken bones that one might suffer as a result of ocean adventure kayaking. Upper-body conditioning and aerobic efficiency allow us to paddle energetically for long periods of time. A limber and resilient body resists injury and recovers more quickly when injuries do occur. Michael practices weight training because of its proven long-term effect on increasing bone density and strength and helping the body withstand the stresses of such experiences as being catapulted end over end in heavy surf. Strong legs, from weight training, hill climbing, and jujitsu,

Paddlers warm up for surf kayaking by doing judo throws.

if it happens at sea or along a remote coast far from help. Some paddlers have learned how to put a displaced shoulder back in place, a valuable skill. Unfortunately, once a shoulder has dislocated, there seems to be increased risk that it could happen again, which is added motivation to practice the exercises that may prevent injury in the first

Dennis Kuhr punches through the shore break.

enable us to more safely carry our boats and gear over rough terrain and up steep slopes when portaging, a common occurrence in wilderness paddling and a leading cause of back strains.

Tendonitis of the wrist sometimes plagues long-distance paddlers. The chance of this painful affliction developing can be reduced by stretching and warming up before kayaking, using a lightweight, feathered paddle, and not gripping your paddle shaft too tightly. Remember to relax and occasionally flex your wrists to neutralize the effects of constantly extending them back while paddling. Wrist-stretching exercises should be incorporated into your workout routine.

The shoulders are the conduit through which a tremendous amount of energy is exchanged back and forth between the body and the sea. The shoulder is a very mobile joint, but a degree of vulnerability comes with that capability. Rotator cuff injuries, once they appear, can be painful and linger for years. Regular stretching and weight training (a good personal trainer can be invaluable here) help prevent injury and encourage the healing process if injuries do occur.

For a paddler, shoulder dislocation can be catastrophic

place. Also, avoid the extreme high brace entirely, even though it looks dramatic in photos. Sports medicine specialists have found that once the arm is extended and rotated back and above the head, it takes very little pressure to pull a shoulder out of place. Especially in heavy surf or around rocks, a good rule is to always keep the elbows bent and in close to the body. We discuss braces later in this chapter.

Some folks experience lower back pain while paddling

a kayak. There was a time when bed rest was prescribed for backaches. Now many sports medicine practitioners are discovering that muscle flaccidity, caused by lack of proper exercise, is a major contributor to many lower back problems. Strong, well-toned abdominal muscles are essential to keeping the lower back in proper alignment and maintaining proper posture. Isometric contraction of the transverse abdominus and the obliques (bridging) keeps the belly supple and strong. Cardiovascular conditioning (running, cycling, cross-country skiing, paddling) discourages excess fat from accumulating around the midsection. Back massage, especially deep tissue work, may also help relieve spasms and increase the healing blood supply.

The severity of injuries caused by violent contact with rocks and other boats can be mitigated by using proper safety equipment, such as helmets, PFDs, and other body armor. Of course, it's best to avoid situations that *cause* these injuries, if possible. Later in this chapter and throughout the book we discuss procedures and the proper use of equipment that will minimize the probability and consequences of collision and other injury-causing situations.

In ocean adventure kayaking, like other extreme sports, one must accept occasional trauma as one of the risks of the game. Actually, the probability of suffering serious injury is less on the water than in many land-based activities, notably mountain climbing, mountain biking, skating, hang gliding, and contact sports such as rugby. But because kayak-related injuries often occur in remote areas and in water, it's important to be well prepared to minimize the risks. The more paddlers in a group possessing wilderness first-aid skills, the better.

Mental Toughness

The mind must also be exercised to avoid injury, make the body work properly, and handle psychological hazards every bit as dangerous as hazards in the environment (which we discuss in the next chapter). First we look at the proper mental attitude and then at pitfalls for the mind.

The Gung Ho Spirit

As with any real adventure, those who seek out the thrills and excitement of extreme-condition ocean kayaking will sooner or later come face to face with personal demons. Extreme sea kayaking, like martial arts or religion, becomes a path toward personal fulfillment, with self-realization as an additional and sometimes unexpected benefit. We reach a deeper understanding of ourselves as we become more skilled and confident paddlers, just as we gain knowledge of the weather and tides by personal interaction with the sea. Any sport where one ventures into a wild, unknown, and sometimes dangerous realm takes real courage, and that courage comes from deep within. If we can't face ourselves, how can we hope to face a wave in a cave?

In the *Star Wars* movies, Jedi Master Yoda proclaims, "Don't try. Do, or don't do." The analogy holds true for ocean kayakers, just as it does for soldiers and mountain climbers. When great warriors advance into battle, they either tri-

Split-second timing and a bit of courage are needed to launch through rocks into breaking surf.

umph or die. If they merely "try," they will probably fail—
and may suffer a coward's death in the bargain. Serious
climbers, facing extremes of altitude and weather, don't just
"try" to make a summit in a half-hearted way. They do—or
they retreat to base camp. They don't climb halfheartedly. It
must be the same for a paddler who dares to enter a powerful surf zone for the first time, or who ventures alone down
a remote and unfamiliar coastline. Either do it, or don't do it.

Initiative and determination are mental qualities that
empower a kayaker to paddle in extreme conditions. *Initiative*, fueled by a thirst for adventure, energizes us to acquire the needed skills and face those first little waves.
Determination will sustain us when we face larger waves
breaking over rocks and into sea caves.

Many extreme sea kayakers are also drawn to martial
arts. In both spheres, mental concentration and *decisiveness*
are crucial. To survive in a tiny craft in an angry sea, you
must train your mind to be calm and receptive under
stress; then you must act decisively and without reservation. In the event of capsize, equipment breakdown, or
other calamity, it's reassuring to know you can remain focused and be decisive. When a break appears between
huge sets of waves and there are only seconds to advance
through the surf zone to shore, there is no time for indeci-
sion and doubt. You must commit yourself wholeheartedly.

Allison Chase
braces physically
and mentally for
challenging
conditions.

Psychological Hazards

**Psychological shortcomings, compared to physical
ones, can be subtle and difficult to define. Though
rarely addressed in paddling literature, the psychological side of kayaking, especially in extreme conditions, merits serious consideration. Here are a
few psycho-gremlins one might encounter in the
sea and some suggestions for dealing with them.**

Fear and Panic in Las Vortex

**We've all heard the old saw about there being
nothing to fear but fear itself. Yet, anyone who has
ever ventured out into the sea on a stormy day
will agree that it can get mighty scary out there.
Obviously, not all fearful reactions are bad. With
experience we gain the ability to discriminate
between irrational, mind-numbing hysteria and
life-giving, vitalizing fear. An excessive or inappropriate fear reaction can short-circuit our energy,
just when we need it most. When we are face-to-
face with real danger, feelings of fear can trigger
massive releases of adrenaline and instantly prepare us for explosive action. A burst of superhu-
man energy may be just what it takes to punch
through an oncoming wave or escape the imaginary *balrog* (a demon from Tolkien's *Lord of the
Rings*) lurking at the back of a dark sea cave.**

Suddenly facing a buildup of wind or breaking waves or
the imminent threat of being dashed onto the rocks can
knot up your stomach, turn your hands to ice, cause trem-
bling throughout the body, and cessation of all rational
thought. "Fear is the mind killer," mused Paul in Frank Her-
bert's *Dune*. An excess of trepidation can render one help-
less and ineffective, just when the car stalls on the tracks
and decisive action is needed desperately. Fear can creep
up slowly, much like the advance of a dark storm front
across the sea, building in intensity with each flash of lightning. Or it can pounce suddenly, like the heart-stopping
moment when Michael mistook a big sea lion bull that burst
to the surface beside his kayak for a great white shark.

If you feel panic building as you approach a surf zone or
the entrance to a sea cave, it may help to visualize yourself

making it through, stroke by stroke. Acknowledge the worst that could happen (you could get wet and pummeled) and view that as part of the fun. Acknowledge the demons lurking there in the shadows; then banish them from sight. Breathe deeply, calm yourself, and get centered.

There's probably nothing worse than facing a fearful situation alone. It helps to seek out the company of others, preferably more skilled and experienced than yourself, with whom to paddle (more on this in chapter 9, "Power of the Tribe"). Don't be afraid to share your fears with your paddling companions. Getting out in the sea together as often as possible will help you face your fears and build confidence. A mountain climber once said, "Those who remain below, know not what is above. But those who climb, know both what is above and below."

Before launching upon a storm-tossed sea, one or another of the Tsunami Rangers will traditionally call out a warrior's mantra such as "Geronimo!" When spoken with spirit and conviction, the mantra dispels fear and replaces it with confidence.

What Happened?

In Aldous Huxley's *Island*, mynah birds fly around the island squawking, "Pay attention!" Spacing out in the midst of a dangerous situation, such as those frequently encountered in extreme-condition sea kayaking, is an insidious psychological hazard, more common than many paddlers realize. In a typical scenario, the kayaker moves through a potentially hazardous environment, such as a rock garden or reef area, with mind cast adrift as the body autopilots. Gazing into the swirling blue waters ahead, the mesmerized paddler may be unaware of a rogue wave bearing down swiftly and silently from behind. By the time the stern of one's kayak starts skyrocketing, it's too late to take defensive action.

Never allow the beauty or apparent peacefulness of the marine environment to lull you into complacency, especially when paddling in a surf zone or rock garden. Powerful natural forces are constantly interacting here, with unpredictable and sometimes explosive results. To paddle safely in the exposed sea, one must continually encourage that mental myna to issue the klaxon "Pay Attention."

In *Stranger in a Strange Land*, Robert Heinlein uses the word *grok* to describe an expanded state of consciousness in which the mind achieves total awareness of everything in an instant. To grok is like the Tao, the ideal extreme sea kayaking state, where you remain in the moment, poised to respond instantly, without distraction or the expenditure of excess mental or physical energy.

I Ain't Scared of Nothin'

On the water, excessive bravado can be as deadly as inattention. Needing to prove something, getting impatient, forgoing common sense, or otherwise losing your center when paddling can cause needless danger to yourself and others. One way to neutralize these self-destructive tendencies is to remain mindful that the ocean is infinitely bigger and more powerful than yourself and can never be dominated or defeated. True power comes not through conquest but by *alignment*, by becoming one with the power, with the flow. Egoism, when it arises, must be gently but firmly put aside. There is no room for machismo on the water.

By returning, time and again, to our great teacher the sea, we learn to discriminate between feelings of zeal and courage, essential when facing surf zones and exposed coasts, and mere hubris. Yet, when things get really exciting out there, when the water turns wild and the wind shrieks, someone is apt to exclaim, "Let's go for it!" Otherwise, we'd remain on the beach, there would be no extreme-condition kayaking, and life would be tame.

Survival Swimming

Being in good shape and having a realistic but positive attitude are rudiments for any rigorous outdoor activity. For extreme sea kayaking, certain proficiencies will make your trips much safer. First and foremost is good swimming skill, for which no PFD can substitute. Poor swimmers will always be

Day of Reckoning

In mid-February 1993, an epic winter storm had whipped up the eastern Pacific like a gigantic blender. One day during this period, the Tsunami Rangers and a National Geographic Explorer film crew were rafted up in their kayaks, just outside a surf zone on the Big Sur coast. We had led the filmmakers down the rugged coast to one of our favorite haunts, where great stone cliffs spilled straight into the sea and formed a labyrinth of sea caves approachable only by kayak. Until then the Rangers had kept the exact location of this place a closely guarded secret, but now we'd promised Geographic we would paddle into those caves for their cameras. Yet, none of us could recall ever seeing such chaos as that created by those colossal waves as they broke and exploded at the mouths of the dark orifices that day. It was as if the gods were angry with us for revealing their lair. After waiting an hour for a break in the surf that never came, we knew that to paddle into those caves would be suicidal. Humbled, we backed away and told the film crew that the conditions were beyond our skill and risk levels. But we were undaunted. We paddled a few hundred yards to the south and discovered another, less exposed sea cave that provided all the action the National Geographic crew desired.

Had we gone into the caves to "prove" ourselves, we might have been badly injured or worse. But we demurred and acknowledged that Shakespeare's Falstaff was right: discretion is the better part of valor.

—Michael

The Tsunami Rangers just go for it in the surf and rocks.

a liability to themselves and others in rough seas, afraid of capsizing, fearful when conditions become more extreme, and hindered when learning more advanced techniques. When paddling around surf and rocks, you must always be physically and mentally prepared to swim. After all, ocean adventure paddling is an *in-water* sport.

To enroll in the Tsunami Rangers' "Paddling the Open Coast" workshop, prospective students demonstrate they can swim 300 meters in 15 minutes or less wearing the protective clothing described in chapter 2—and still paddle for the rest of the day. The reason is simple: when paddling in extreme conditions, it's not uncommon to end up in a survival swimming situation where you may be on your own with 300 meters between you and safety.

In the Swim of Things

Imagine you enter a surf zone, are caught inside, and are wiped out by a big, thumping wave. Suddenly you find yourself separated from your boat. What would you do? Everything looks and feels very different now. But thanks to your wetsuit and PFD, you are warm and buoyant, which helps you remain calm and assess your situation. Your washdeck boat is floating nearby, and you still have your paddle. If a lull appears between sets, you simply swim a few strokes back to the boat and remount. If the surf is raging, you let the boat wash in on its own, and you swim and body-surf to shore. Don't signal other paddlers to approach and assist you in big surf, unless absolutely necessary. Another boat nearby in breaking waves could hit you, making the situation worse. It's better to remain on your own and save yourself than to be rescued.

If a big wave approaches and begins to break over you, dive beneath it (admittedly tough to do while wearing a PFD) and resurface after it has passed. You can increase your forward momentum by stroking with your paddle, much as you would if you were in your boat. If you catch a wave and begin body-surfing, bring your paddle in line with your body position with the forward blade horizontal on the surface in front of you, like a mini-boogie board.

Another place kayakers frequently end up swimming is in an ocean rock garden. If this happens to you when breaking waves and powerful currents are present, it may be better to swim back out toward the open sea where your companions can safely assist you. Leave your boat to be towed out by the other paddlers and save yourself by swimming out. If that proves infeasible, look for an opportunity to mimic the seals and ride the surge up onto a flat ledge or rock. To accomplish a seal landing safely, timing and positioning are crucial. Wait for a moderate-sized wave and then swim forward energetically, allowing the water to lift you. When you have drifted up as high on the rock as the wave can take you, grab on with your hands and feet until the wave has receded; then scramble upward until you are out of danger. We discuss more swimming techniques, including swimming rescues, in subsequent chapters.

Preparing for Life on a Water Planet

Lap swimming is one way to maintain your swimming skills and can be practiced throughout the seasons in a heated pool. If you're not yet a proficient swimmer, a **YMCA, American**

A Swim from Hell

A few years ago, a small group of us gathered at Moss Beach on the northern California coast at the onset of a big storm. Captain Jim Kakuk decided to take an intermediate paddler named Nick out with him in his Tsunami X-2 washdeck double kayak. Mindful of the weather, they intended to remain in what appeared to be a relatively safe area inside the reef. I agreed to accompany them in my single kayak and lend assistance if necessary. Just 100 meters from shore, we found ourselves in 50-knot winds and 20-foot visibility and soon became separated. I immediately sensed we were in trouble.

Soon, a big wave roared over the reef and capsized the double. Jim and Nick struggled to reach a sea stack, where Jim assisted his partner in clambering up out of immediate danger. Jim then returned to his swamped boat and tried to push it into a nearby cove, but the rebounding force of the big storm seas made that impossible. At last, Jim was forced to abandon the boat and swim for shore. However, the sleeves of the paddle jacket he had borrowed that day had filled with water, weighing him down. Each swimming stroke drove Jim to the brink of exhaustion.

Meanwhile, I had fought my way back to the "safe" zone to find no sign of Jim and Nick. In the flying spray, I could only see a few feet in front of me. I started to paddle where I thought Jim and Nick might be but had a change of heart. I spun my kayak around and paddled away from the maelstrom and back to the beach, where I found fellow Rangers John Lull and John Dixon waiting anxiously. Fearing the worst, we bounded along the rocky shoreline, searching for our companions. We spotted Nick, clinging to a rock offshore like a storm-beaten palm frond.

Dixon swam out to Nick and coaxed him back into the water. Dixon and Lull then assisted Nick in reaching the safety of the beach. I continued sprinting up the beach, looking everywhere for Jim. At last, I spotted a crumpled form crawling out of the surf, like an injured seal. It was Jim. As I drew near, I could see his waxen face and knew he was very weak. I half-carried him up the beach to my house. Some warm broth and a soak in the hot tub revitalized both Jim and Nick.

Once again, the sea had taught us a hard lesson. Even though we had been a strong team, equipped with the proper boats and gear for extreme conditions, we had made a basic error in judgment in underestimating the ferocious power of the storm. Jim reflected that while he was fighting for his life in the sea, he felt very tired and alone, but he just kept going, determined not to give up. We were all reminded of how important it is to be in good shape and keep honing those swimming skills. It was a while before Jim ventured back into big surf, and that was the last time Nick ever went out with the Tsunami Rangers.

—Eric

Red Cross, or other swimming course will provide you with the basics and help you build confidence. If you are fortunate to live near the sea, swimming and body-surfing in the surf zone is wonderful exercise and excellent preparation for ocean kayaking. You will build skill and stamina and will also gain experience dealing with wave dynamics and currents. In addition, swimming in the sea is free and great fun.

Different Strokes for Different Folks

The next essential set of skills are paddling strokes. There are many bluewater kayaking books, such as *The Essential Sea Kayaker* by David Seidman (see chapter 11, "Resources"), that explain basic paddling techniques in detail. We present here a review of the subject and comment on the strokes as they apply to extreme sea kayaking. We omit a description of paddling techniques for touring or racing on flat water but include relevant strokes used by whitewater river paddlers.

Forward, Back, Side to Side

The basic maneuver for forward propulsion is the *power* stroke. The paddle shaft is gripped firmly but not tightly with the hands about shoulder width apart. First one blade and then the other are drawn back smoothly alongside the boat. When you need sudden acceleration to punch through an oncoming wave, lean forward, keep your head down, and push the balls of your feet against your pedals or foot pegs. Your strokes can now become rapid, like when a boxer works out with a speed bag. Put your whole body behind each stroke, making your legs and hips contribute to the quick bursts of power that your arms deliver to the paddle. This technique is also useful when you want to catch a wave or escape from some peril. Short, quick strokes work best when you are maneuvering through tight

quarters, such as a rock garden or sea cave. Bring your paddle out of the water as it comes alongside your waist; don't follow through as much as you would if you were touring on the open sea. In kayak surfing and rock garden play, you always have to be ready to change strokes instantaneously.

In the *sweep* stroke, the paddle is pulled in a wide arc around the boat, either forward or in reverse, causing it to pivot on its axis and effect a quick change in direction. A sweep stroke combined with *sculling*, where the paddle blade is swept along the surface with its leading edge higher like an airplane wing, provides a sustained lifting effect that can push a half-capsized paddler back upright. A partial sweep stroke, where you start at the stern or bow and sweep out about ten degrees, is called a *rudder* stroke and is used to turn or correct your boat's course in following seas (stern rudder) or to back surf (bow rudder).

Backstrokes, basically power strokes in reverse, serve a function in ocean whitewater. They can help a paddler get into position in the surf zone or back out of a bad situation without turning the boat around.

The draw and pry strokes work equally well in kayak surfing and rock garden play. The *draw* stroke is used to move your boat sideways to get to a better position. To execute it, place your paddle out to the side toward which you wish to travel, with the blade parallel to your boat, and pull on the paddle so the boat moves toward it. The pry is used for the same purpose and is performed just the opposite of the draw. To pry, put your

Gordon Brown, high bracing in surf and rocks.

blade next to the side of your hull away from which you wish to paddle, with the blade parallel to your boat, and push the paddle away from the boat.

Other techniques developed by whitewater river kayakers and canoeists, such as the paddle brace, are used in extreme ocean conditions. The *paddle brace* is similar to the draw stroke, except instead of stroking you lean on the paddle once it's away from the boat. The brace is used when broaching in surf. Remember to keep your elbows close to your sides when bracing so you don't dislocate your shoulders.

Slalom maneuvers in the sea require combining the paddling strokes discussed above. The secret is to practice, practice, practice, preferably in wild water, until these responses become reflexive. When paddling in extreme conditions, if you have to stop and think about what to do, it's usually too late.

Misha Dynnikov works to gain control of his kayak in a suckhole.

Ninja Strokes

We borrowed the term *ninja* strokes from William Nealy's book *Kayak* to describe a paddling system used in ocean whitewater, especially in rock gardens and sea caves (see chapter 11, "Resources"). They are called ninja strokes because they resemble a series of martial arts moves—quick, decisive, acrobatic. The following scenario illustrates how ninja strokes work.

Suppose you are lined up with a big rock in a surf zone and a 6-foot wave approaches out of the open sea. You might nimbly back-paddle into takeoff position and unleash two or three power strokes to explode forward and meet the wave, followed by a quick bow rudder to correct your course. Then in rapid succession could come a pivoting draw, half a forward sweep, and a slap stroke to regain balance, a low brace, which turns into another power stroke, a quick pry to avoid a rock, and two backstrokes and a back sweep to brake and turn the boat around. A low brace, a sculling draw, a series of rapid power strokes, and a stern rudder enable you to escape through the back door of the rock garden just as a monster wave comes billowing in from outside.

As you continue to paddle in extreme conditions and refine your skills, the ninja style and feeling will begin to feel natural to you. To thrive in ocean whitewater, learn to paddle reflexively, without conscious effort, just as martial arts masters defend themselves in a fight. Ninja strokes, executed properly in cadence with the tremendous power of an aroused sea, are invaluable survival tools and beautiful to watch.

Mastering the Three Rs: Roll, Recovery, Rescue

Self-rescue is another basic and essential paddling skill addressed in every book on basic sea kayaking. We discuss self-rescue here to underscore its importance. Let's start with your first line of defense, the bombproof roll.

Rock 'n Roll

To paddle with safety and confidence in ocean whitewater, you must roll reliably, especially in the worst conditions. Without a good roll, you will find yourself avoiding surfing or other advanced maneuvers because you fear capsizing. Capsizing is a normal occurrence in whitewater, sometimes even self-initiated to avoid collision.

Master sea kayaker Derek Hutchinson deemed the Eskimo roll such an important skill that he devoted an entire book to it (see chapter 11, "Resources"). If you are determined enough, you can probably learn to roll on your own or with the help of a friend—we both self-taught ourselves to roll by trial and error. However, it is easier, quicker, and better to complete a roll class where trained instructors will work with you in a pool. The trick then is to transfer these newfound skills to the surf zone.

There are many subtle variations on the rolling theme. Most of the Tsunami Rangers and other extreme sea kayakers tend to favor the *screw roll*, so named because you "screw" yourself up to the surface and back into an upright position by a smooth, spiraling motion. This is the essential roll to master, along with the *hand roll*, which is handy when you've become separated from your paddle. When executed properly, the screw roll can be accomplished quickly and powerfully, a decided advantage in an emergency situation.

Michael has found that wearing a diver's mask while practicing underwater maneuvers enables students to see everything clearly. Eric believes it is best to keep your eyes closed when learning to roll so you get used to the feel of it. Experiment and see which approach works for you.

To set up for the screw roll, bend your body forward with your face close to the front deck and your paddle held parallel along the side of the boat. Whitewater river runners discovered an added benefit of this position is the protection it offers the head and upper torso while hurtling along upside down over rocks in a swift current. Be certain the paddle is up on the surface alongside the kayak, and then begin sculling it across the surface toward the stern of the boat. Stay relaxed and allow the head and body to naturally follow as you sweep the paddle around. As the force exerted by the sculling blade begins to rotate the kayak, added impetus is gained by snapping the hips in the same direction you are rotating. The head and upper body should spiral far forward and then upright, leaving the head in the water until the boat

is completely righted. Raising the head too soon is a common mistake. The protruding weight will counteract the upright momentum, and you will capsize again. But don't be discouraged. With practice, rolling upright in a kayak becomes about as effortless as turning over in bed.

Another screw-type roll is the *layback roll*, which you do when slammed onto your back deck. The trick is to lie supine and keep your head on the deck until the roll is completed. The layback position makes it easy to perform a hand roll, should you misplace or break your paddle.

In addition to perfecting the screw roll, it's worthwhile to learn the *recovery slap*, which works like this: when thrown off balance suddenly, slap or scull your paddle blade energetically on the water surface and snap your hips to rotate yourself back to upright position. In effect, your paddle is bouncing off the water as if it were a trampoline.

If you capsize in shallow water, as on a reef, *pole vault* off the bottom. Just place the tip of your paddle against the bottom and use it for support as you vault back to an upright position, remembering to snap your hips in the direction of rotation and to leave your head in the water until your boat is completely upright.

The Recovery Room

In a pond or protected lagoon, you can learn to roll at your leisure, and failing to do so repeatedly is of little consequence. However, paddling into an ocean rock garden or sea cave, especially when powerful surf is present, becomes a more serious undertaking. A capsize here puts the head and upper torso at serious risk, as both authors can well testify (see the photo on page 18 of chapter 2 showing Michael with a bloody head after his helmet was torn off in heavy turbulence, and he struck the reef with his head). If you are thrown upside down in shallow water and unable to roll up quickly, bail out without delay (make a *wet exit*). To hesitate is to risk getting knocked out or otherwise incapacitated. Even if you live through the experience, you will have to explain to friends how you got those striations across your face. Assuming you are properly dressed for immersion, you are much safer swimming than hanging upside down in your kayak.

Once you have bailed out and are swimming, you may still be able to recover on your own, as distinguished from being rescued by others. *Rescue* implies you are a victim who needs saving. *Recovery*, or self-rescue, is a procedure you accomplish unassisted and is preferred.

If you are paddling a sit-on-top kayak, such as the Tsunami X-15, recovery is a simple affair. Merely swim over to your boat and slither back on. This is accomplished by doing a frog or side kick while you slide your chest across the cockpit until you are looking down at the water on the other side of the kayak. Move your hips into position over the seat depression, rotate into a sitting position, swing your feet back to the rudder pedals, and you are ready to go. If you paddle a washdeck kayak, practice this *remounting* procedure until you can do it nearly as fast as you can roll.

With a conventional closed-cockpit kayak, there are two options available to a paddler who has come out of the boat in a surf zone. The first is to swim toward shore, pushing the waterlogged kayak along or trusting that the wind and waves will return it to shallow water. This is the easiest but most time-consuming and ego-deflating option.

Your second option is the *reentry and roll* technique, which can be performed during a lull in the waves or on open water. After exiting the capsized craft, wait until conditions settle down, as this procedure will take several seconds. Holding onto your paddle, take a deep breath, dive beneath the still upturned boat and wiggle back into the kayak. If possible, reset your spray skirt back onto the coaming; then roll up. Less water will get into your cockpit this way; more water will make paddling difficult. If you run out of air before you can reattach your skirt, roll up first and then attach it. Pump the water out of your boat as soon as it is safe.

There are other complicated methods of self-rescue utilizing paddle floats of various types, but the reentry and roll is best because it is based on your skill and not on gear that must be found, inflated, and attached in the same conditions that just caused your capsize.

To the Rescue

If you are paddling a conventional closed-cockpit boat and self-rescue in the surf zone is not an option, hold onto your boat and frog kick it into a relatively calm area where there are no breaking waves. At the same time, attract the attention of your paddling companions by shouting and waving your paddle above your head. They can then assist you. The standard assisted rescue method for closed-cockpit boats is the *rafted T*, as described by Derek Hutchinson in his books. The advantage of the rafted T is it can be accomplished with only one rescue boat. Both the swimmer and the paddler(s) assist in getting the upside-down boat up onto and across the rescue kayak's foredeck (this should look like a letter *T*), so that most of the water will drain out. Then the boat is returned to an upright position and held alongside the rescue kayak by gripping the cowling of its cockpit and laying a paddle across the decks of both boats to keep them rafted up together. The swimmer then crawls up and reenters the boat, pumps or bails out any remaining water, and resecures the spray skirt. Rescue and recovery procedures should be rehearsed diligently *before* paddling into breaking surf and rock conditions where they will most likely become required.

You can practice essential skills like recovery, rescue, rolling, paddle strokes, and swimming in a local pool if it is not convenient to go to the beach. You can cross-train and prepare your body for paddling in extreme conditions in any number of land-based activities. And you can work on your mental attitude in every activity you do. In chapter 4, we discuss what to expect when you go out on the mighty sea.

4

The Mighty Sea

> " The places of the sea and the land change. There is no place on earth always land nor always sea. "
>
> —El-Mas'udi, Arabic geographer, A.D. 950

Some things do not change. For thousands of years, kayaking has been a way of experiencing the power, meeting the elusive residents, and discovering the breathtaking beauty that lies beyond the shores of our water world. From the cockpit of such a craft, a minimum of technology stands between us and the marine environment. Yet from such an intimate perspective, the sea at times seems capricious, even cruel. The more extreme the conditions into which we dare to venture, the more important it is that we really *know* the sea and its inhabitants. With this deeper understanding comes increased confidence and skill and the freedom to venture forth into the mighty sea.

Sea Sense

Climbers who spend enough time outdoors in extreme alpine environments inevitably begin to gain a sense of attunement to the mountains that transcends the ordinary intellectual level of understanding. The same is true for sea kayakers and others who devote themselves to learning about the ocean

world. Sea sense is not something that can be taught in books or schools. One must go directly to the University of the Sea for these lessons.

Though a poor substitute for ocean experience, we use this chapter to present basic information for kayakers about the sea. First we cover the "three Ws": reading wind, weather, and waves. Next we tell you how to deal with two of the sea's top hazards—hypothermia and sea creatures. Then we discuss when to use objective,

Kayakers approach Mavericks Reef in northern California.

subjective, and intuitive navigation—and how to navigate at night. Finally, we introduce scouting, an activity that ties together everything in this chapter.

Reading Wind

Expert sea kayaker Derek Hutchinson refers to wind as the ocean kayaker's "greatest enemy." Unquestionably, the effects of wind velocity and direction are very noticeable to a person at sea. Holding up a wet finger to feel which side feels cool is a time-tested way to determine the direction from which the wind is coming. The speed of the wind is revealed more by visual clues. For example, Eric encountered a group of paragliders in Wyoming and was impressed by how closely his intuitive estimates of the wind speed, based on movement of tree branches, matched the readings of the paragliders' electronic anemometer.

On the sea, whitecaps become visible when the wind reaches the Beaufort Wind Scale of about Force 5. At this point, inexperienced sea kayakers should get off the water immediately. When light spray is evident, wind speed Force 6, you enter the realm of extreme-condition sea kayaking. Paddling into winds this strong can be tiring, but an experienced paddler can attain good speed when heading downwind. At Force 7–8 spindrift blows off the tops of waves, and making headway becomes problematical for all but the ablest kayaker. This is truly extreme sea kayaking. Winds of 47 mph and above (Force 9–10) can blow a strong person down like a fire hose spraying on a rioter —*extremely* extreme sea kayaking. This table

shows the Beaufort Scale with associated wind speeds (in statute mph) and sea state.

When setting out to kayak, look for wind signs on the water. Then decide if you are up to the conditions. If you are inexperienced, don't go out if the local seas are covered with whitecaps (Force 5) because conditions often worsen as the day goes on or intensify around a point. Don't take unnecessary risks. Baja sea kayaking guide Kenny Howell studies the sky and the horizon carefully and won't risk leading a group of clients out onto the Sea of Cortez if he suspects a notorious El Norte wind might be approaching.

On the other hand, if you are an experienced kayaker, use the wind to your advantage, as we do. During a typical exploratory paddle along the exposed Pacific coast, the Tsunami Rangers might launch early in the morning when traveling north to avoid the prevailing northwest winds that kick up around noon. Returning south, we may linger in camp until midday to take advantage of the wind at our backs and make great speed with little effort.

"The wind speaks the message of the sun to the sea," writes Drew Kampion in *The Book of Waves* (see chapter 11, "Resources"). Wind is often a major factor in extreme sea kayaking conditions. Kayak surfers welcome an offshore

> "The fair breeze blew, the white foam flew." –Samuel Taylor Coleridge

Beaufort Wind Scale

Beaufort #	Wind Speed (mph)	Wind Term	Sea Conditions
Force 1	1–3	light air	water is barely ruffled
Force 2	4–7	light breeze	noticeable ripples on water
Force 3	8–12	gentle breeze	water is rippled all over; a few whitecaps
Force 4	13–18	moderate breeze	more whitecaps; affects progress
Force 5	19–24	fresh breeze	full of whitecaps; for skilled kayakers only
Force 6	25–31	strong breeze	some spray; small-craft advisories
Force 7	32–38	moderate gale	seas are whipped up; headway is difficult
Force 8	39–46	gale	spray is flying over confused seas
Force 9	47–54	strong gale	spumes and large breaking waves; no headway
Force 10	55–63	whole gale/storm	huge waves and white seas; complete chaos

breeze, as it tends to steepen the oncoming waves and sends beautiful spindrift streaming off the tops of breakers. Wind from distant storms at sea generates the big ocean swells that make for exciting surf conditions. For example, winter storms in Hawaii, the Gulf of Alaska, and off the Mexican coast bring majestic surf to northern California. However, strong local winds generate choppy, confused seas that are not very good for surfing and that make paddling difficult or even dangerous.

John Lull and Eric Soares back up to a rock and face the oncoming waves.

Reading Weather

Air and water temperatures and precipitation, along with wind, greatly influence human safety and comfort at sea. Yet for paddlers who are mentally and physically up to the challenge, wild weather intensifies the drama and excitement of extreme sea kayaking situations.

Long ago, sailors could read the weather by looking at the sky and feeling the changes in air pressure on their bodies. If the sky darkened at midday or their joints ached, they knew a storm was imminent. They did not need instruments to predict weather. In similar manner, satirist

Ambrose Bierce defined *barometer* as "an ingenious instrument which indicates what kind of weather we are having." Some modern instruments, such as waterproof sport watches with built-in compass and weather indicators, are proving useful to modern sea kayakers, who may lack the skills of ancient mariners. Instrument data, correlated with your own observations, help you make crucial decisions, like whether to remain in camp, resume paddling down an exposed coast, or risk an open sea crossing.

If you're an avid sea kayaker, you've probably spent enough time outdoors to gain a good feel for your local climate and how it affects paddling conditions. However, when you arrive in a new locale, before paddling, it's wise to inquire of the locals about what to expect during a particular season. Also, as noted in chapter 2, a VHF radio or marine weather radio serves as yet another way to obtain information about storms, wind, temperature, and wave size.

Be aware of cyclic changes that may affect the weather in the area you wish to paddle. At the time of this writing, for example, the weather along the Pacific coast of North and South America is being influenced profoundly by a climatic phenomenon known as *El Niño*. For reasons that are not entirely understood, warmer sea water from the South Pacific periodically flows east and then north along these coasts, bringing big tropical storms and immense amounts of rainfall to normally dry areas. For several months now, tropical fish, such as barracuda and tuna, have been appearing in California waters. Record catches of albacore and Mexican lobsters have been reported by fishermen, while some local species have all but disappeared. The pleasantly warm water and occasional big south storm waves have been welcomed by local surfers and extreme-condition sea kayakers. However, it is possible for a dangerous tropical storm, even a hurricane, to reach our northern California coast during a cycle such as this.

The bottom line is to use whatever means are available to stay abreast of the imminent and distant weather. Your life may depend on it. The ill-fated, storm-tossed kayak voyage described in "Our Cup Floodeth Over" illustrates the importance of paying attention to the weather and planning and acting accordingly.

Reading Waves

Swells in the open sea differ dramatically from waves breaking near the shore. Waves in deep water are pulses of energy moving through a liquid medium, which remains relatively stationary. However, when that same energy begins to encounter shallow sea bottom, it reacts by piling up, like traffic at rush hour. When the water depth decreases to about 1.5 times the wave height, the rising wave breaks, and its energy is released as the dramatic surf we observe crashing on beaches or among rocks.

Other than rare seismic waves—tsunamis—created by a sudden, massive disturbance of the sea floor (e.g., undersea earthquakes or volcanic eruptions) or the daily rise and fall of tidal action, ocean waves caused by wind are of most interest to sea kayakers. Local breezes can first cause the surface of the sea to ripple and then become increasingly choppy and rough as they increase in intensity. Big storms that occur hundreds or even thousands of miles away and act upon great expanses of open sea (this distance is referred to as *fetch*) form the long, smooth, fast-moving waves called *swells*.

By observing the sea, even on the wildest days, you will note that deep ocean swells arrive in a somewhat organized, rhythmic order. Typically, a series of smaller waves will be regularly punctuated by the arrival of one or more much bigger, more powerful waves. During a storm, the opposite may occur: after a seemingly endless series of big waves, a few smaller ones may arrive, creating a "window of opportunity" for kayakers to launch and punch out through a surf zone.

Our Cup Floodeth Over

Awareness of tides and weather patterns is vitally important for sea kayakers, especially those on extended journeys through the open sea or the exposed coast. Once again, this became evident a few years ago when the Tsunami Rangers converged on the rugged southern Oregon coast for a paddling expedition. As launch time approached, we considered sea and weather conditions carefully. It was drizzling steadily, which was no cause for concern. The tides were increasing daily as the moon waxed toward fullness. The wind and swells were out of the northwest at about 20 knots (Force 5) and 6 feet. There was no apparent current or tidal stream. We listened to the NOAA marine weather broadcast, which predicted scattered storms and an inch of rain over the next 24 hours. What the broadcast didn't tell us was that this front was the vanguard of a series of powerful storms stacked up out in the Pacific, all the way up to the Gulf of Alaska.

Conditions began to intensify soon after we launched from Whaleshead Cove and began paddling up the exposed coast. We forged ahead through lashing headwinds and building waves for about 5 miles until we reached our first campsite, a hidden pocket beach nearly surrounded by high cliffs and inaccessible except from the sea. We had discovered this spot on a previous expedition and named it Cathedral Cove because of the god rays that streamed down here at sunset. But that day the sun was obscured by a phalanx of dark, marching clouds.

Tsunami Rangers play in a suckhole and washover on the Oregon coast.

The stormy weather, though not unusual on the Oregon coast in early autumn, was not exactly welcome. Perhaps we lacked the toughness of the Aleutian kayakers who once paddled this way hunting sea otters. It was easy to imagine them landing upon this very beach, gathering dinner from the sea

(c o n t i n u e d   o n   p a g e   4 0)

(continued from page 39)

as they came. Those aboriginal people of the sea probably put together a drier, warmer camp than ours without a scrap of Gore-Tex or polypro. We envisioned the weathered cliffs above our heads resounding with the sound of voices as they feasted and sang ancient songs around a flickering fire.

Soon after our landing, we realized with alarm that the storm-driven waves, in collusion with the advancing tide, were threatening to inundate the entire beach. We retreated to a precarious perch at the base of the cliffs and nervously set up our tents. Runoff from the rain began cascading down from above, bringing with it impressive quantities of the Oregon mountainside. Everyone set about digging trenches and dikes in the sand with their paddles in a desperate attempt to divert both the freshwater and salt water from our besieged camp. By now darkness was closing in, and returning to the stormy sea was out of the question.

We had just finished dinner and dispersed when an avalanche of mud and rock slid down the cliff and buried our campfire. The rain intensified, and the waterfalls streaming down the cliffs grew more powerful. A fortunate few of us were able to crowd into two shallow caves at the base of the cliffs, while the others retreated to their sodden tents. The storm raged on through the night, rocks continued to crash down, and the rising tide overcame our dikes and lapped against the edges of the tents. When dawn came at last, it revealed a beach swept clean by the hungry surf, which had now grown to the height of a football goalpost. We scrambled to break camp and ready the kayaks before the next high tide arrived. After repeated efforts, everyone was able to punch through the big breaking waves, and we fled up the coast to higher ground.

Being trapped that night at Cathedral Cove taught us a few lessons we will never forget, as well as some new survival skills. When we paddle on exposed coasts now during stormy weather, we choose our campsites carefully. We always have an emergency evacuation plan in place, especially when we overnight on a pocket beach when high tides and big seas are present.

were paddling an 8-foot wave ski, it would fit lengthwise on the wave.

Waves approaching land break in different ways. A *surging* wave occurs where deep water reaches all the way to shore (as against a steep cliff face), allowing no opportunity for oncoming waves to build up and break. Here, wave energy is expressed instead as a sudden upwelling, or surge. By contrast, when the sea bottom slopes up very gradually, a *spilling* wave results. Where the sea bottom inclines at a moderate angle, the crests of waves (especially larger waves) are hurled forward, resulting in *plunging* waves, sometimes with a spectacular hollow tube forming along their

Kayakers in whitewater river boats surf at La Push in winter swells.

face. Smaller, spilling waves are ideal for learning to surf with a kayak, whereas steeper, plunging waves offer great challenge and excitement for kayakers with more skill and experience.

The common *beach break* occurs when waves encounter a fairly smooth shoreline with a sloping sand or gravel bottom. Because this material is moved around over time by water movement, wave patterns may change here, particularly during the winter storm season. *Rip currents*, created when channels form where the spent surf rushes back away from shore, can appear un-

A wave has measurable length (distance between it and the other waves) and height (vertical distance), a trough, and a crest. The amount of time between waves is called the *period*. These facts are of interest to kayakers. For example, the first question asked when someone is telling a surfing story is, "How *high* were the waves?" Sometimes, they might want to know how long the wave face was. You might reply that the wave height was 4 feet and the wave face was 9 feet, which means that if you

expectedly along beach breaks. Dumping waves, a hazard to swimmers and boaters, often develop here. However, when swell size and direction, wind, and bottom conditions mesh, good surfing conditions can occasionally be found along beach breaks.

A *reef break* results when solid rock or coral rises up to form a shallow barrier over which oncoming swells must pass. Banzai Pipeline on Oahu's north shore, a coral reef break, has long been a mecca for big-wave board surfers. Mavericks, on the northern California coast, is a classic rock reef break, infamous for the plunging megawaves it sometimes generates.

A *point break* occurs where waves refract, or wrap around a protruding point of land before breaking. Some reef and point breaks are ideal for kayak surfing because they offer a nice deep-water zone in which the wave can dissipate its leftover energy after breaking. This is the ocean equivalent of a quiet pool below a rapid in a whitewater river, a safe place in which an out-of-control kayaker may recover. Also, reef and point breaks usually have *shoulders* where water depth on each side of the wave decreases gradually and the size and intensity of the breaking waves diminishes, affording the less experienced or less confident kayaker a safer, more mellow zone in which to surf. If a wave breaking upon a point encounters deep water again, it will dissipate, allowing a broaching or capsized kayaker an opportunity to regain control.

We discuss the ideal

Gordon Brown battles his way through the surf at Pillar Point.

wave in the next chapter on kayak surfing. For now, we turn to two dangers of the sea: hypothermia, the most common cause of death of sea kayakers, and sea creatures, the most feared threat in the sea.

Sea Hazards

Besides drowning, getting skewered by another boat, collisions with rocks, and unintentionally getting caught inside a nasty surf zone (or, worse yet, in a sea cave by big breaking waves), the two dangers of hypothermia and marine animals are of concern to extreme sea kayakers. Let's take an in-depth look at hypothermia, the most common hazard.

Hypothermia

Unless they are paddling in the tropics, the greatest threat facing sea kayakers is immersion in cold water. Unlike sailors, who have warm, dry places in which to retreat, paddlers pay for the freedom and simplicity of their existence by becoming much more exposed to the elements. The unfortunate result is that hypothermia (lowering of the body's core temperature to dangerous levels) kills more sea kayakers than all other hazards combined. Paddlers who venture out in extreme conditions *will* capsize, and those not adequately clothed and experienced in rescue techniques become an instant liability to themselves and to the rest of their group.

In cold or even cool water (below 70°F), a wetsuit of sufficient thickness buys a capsized paddler precious time (see chapter 2 for details on wetsuit combinations). In arctic waters, a drysuit, worn over insulating layers of polypro or wool, becomes a critically important line of defense against the sudden and deadly effects of immersion. The reason is simple: water conducts heat away from the body 20 times faster than air. *Wind chill*, the dramatic increase in the cooling effect of cold air in motion, is also dangerous. If the air temperature is 50°F, a wind speed of 20 mph will

Jaime Prado dodges rocks in the cold surf of southern Chile.

cause heat to convect away from your body as if the actual air temperature was 32° F—freezing!

Even wearing a full wetsuit and insulating garments does not ensure that an immersed paddler will not eventually suffer the effects of exposure. Failing to ingest sufficient high-calorie food or water, becoming exhausted, getting sick or injured, taking medications, being anxious or emotionally stressed, or simply remaining inert too long can increase vulnerability to cold. Slender individuals or those with circulation problems may also suffer excessively from the effects of low temperature. A combination of these factors can lead to hypothermia within minutes.

If you find yourself or others beginning to get cold while kayaking, put on more layers and try paddling harder. If this doesn't work, head for shore, get into dry clothing and even a sleeping bag and tent, or build a fire if needed. If a person in your party exhibits signs of severe hypothermia, he or she may require immediate medical attention. It is life threatening to move the victim in this condition yourself, so keep the victim as warm as possible and call an air or sea rescue ambulance.

For those who desire to learn more about prevention and treatment of hypothermia, read William Forgey's *Hypothermia* (see chapter 11, "Resources"). As with most marine hazards, prevention is paramount. Most hypothermia can be avoided by dressing properly for conditions. Then acquire the necessary skills, experience, and good judgment that will help you avoid dangerous situations and deal with capsizing effectively, should it occur.

Hazardous Marine Animals

Another potential hazard, more imagined than real, comes in the form of sea animals, also known as sea monsters, leviathans, and the like. For the most part, sea creatures are not out to get humans, but this is not always the case. The following kayaker - sea animal encounters showcase both danger and splendor.

In the fall of 1992, Ken Kelton and Mike Chin were surfing their kayaks off Año Nuevo Island, about 60 miles south of San Francisco. Año Nuevo is home to a large colony of elephant seals and California and Stellar sea lions, some of

the great white shark's favorite prey. Suddenly, Ken sensed a disturbance in the sea behind him and then felt a tremendous impact to his kayak. As his horrified partner watched, Ken and his slalom kayak were lifted clear out of the water by a great white shark. The huge creature had clamped its jaws over the back of Ken's kayak and proceeded to hold it aloft for several seconds, shaking it like a dog with a bone. The kayak was slammed repeatedly from side to side, while Ken flailed with his paddle, struggling to remain upright. He recalls hearing the scraping sound of the shark's teeth tearing through the plastic deck of the boat behind the cockpit. Then, as suddenly as it had appeared, the shark vanished. Ken and Mike paddled furiously toward shore and managed to land before Ken's lacerated kayak sank.

A white shark's bite in Ken Kelton's kayak.

The two shaken paddlers were staring down at a 17-inch row of teeth marks, plainly visible across the back deck of Ken's red Dancer, when a mounted park ranger rode up, wearing a pistol on her hip and looking very stern. "This is a restricted area. You can't land here," she announced. Then the ranger glanced down at Ken's boat and gasped, "Oh, my God!" Embarrassed, she quietly slipped her citation book back into her saddle bag.

A few months later, a group of kayakers were paddling open-deck boats along the rocky Sonoma County shoreline north of San Francisco when a woman experienced a sharp blow to the underside of her boat. The impact flung her into the air and capsized her. She assumed the blow was caused by coming down upon a submerged rock and was not overly concerned. Her companions, however, had spotted the dorsal fin of a big shark. They yanked her from the water and raced for shore. Later they recovered the woman's "unbreakable" plastic boat, which had a large hole in the bottom where the shark had struck it.

It's encouraging to note that neither of these attacks resulted in injury to a kayaker. This substantiates the belief that sharks commonly take an experimental bite and then swim away if the prey does not react predictably or taste good. Kayakers stand a better chance of surviving shark encounters than do swimmers, divers, or board surfers. Still, if you find yourself in the proximity of a shark or other large marine animal, it's wise to go smoothly and quickly to shore and land. If big surf, a dangerous shoreline, or great distance from land rule out that option, signal your companions to raft up together; a tightly gathered group may appear less vulnerable to a potential aggressor than an individual paddler.

Eric and Jim Kakuk were paddling near Point Reyes in northern California one fine spring day when a giant fin sliced the water surface between the two boaters. At first glance it looked like a prehistoric white shark. *Jaws* turned out to be a rare beaked whale whose beautiful blue eyes gazed at the paddlers in wonder for a few moments before vanishing into the depths.

Another time, Eric and Jim were paddling north of Santa Barbara. They were only a few boat lengths from the sandy cliffs in about 15 feet of water when they spotted a rock moving toward them. "It's a whale!" Jim shouted. By then the huge mammal was only 20 feet away and bearing down on the hapless pair. Eric, on a collision course with the whale, jammed down on his left rudder pedal and executed a reflexive sweep stroke on the right side, sending the bow of his boat scraping over Jim's stern. The 40-foot leviathan, which, like the kayakers, must have been half-asleep, lumbered on, directly over the spot Eric had occupied a split second before.

Besides having their boats munched by great white sharks, kayakers have been charged by sea lion bulls in the Farallon Islands off the northern California coast and by

elephant seals in Patagonia, stared down by huge leopard seals in Tierra del Fuego, fluked by gray whales, and stung by jellyfish and stingrays in Mexico.

Yet, paddlers have also been approached by murrelet chicks who thought the boaters were their mother. The harbor seals at Pillar Point in northern California regularly swim up to greet kayakers, escorted by squadrons of pelicans, surfing by on the air currents inches above the waves. On the Na Pali coast, sea turtles drift by as they have for millennia. Sea otters, floating on their backs among the kelp and serenely munching on crabs and urchins, are a common sight to sea kayakers in Monterey Bay.

Most contact between marine life and humans is harmless and exciting for both species. Still, when you spot any marine animal while on the water, especially a big, potentially dangerous creature, it's prudent and polite to give it a wide berth. In the case of protected species, it is also legally required. The orcas in Robson Bight are not the same as the ones you see being petted by ecstatic children at Marine World. Wherever great white sharks are known to congregate, such as near the Farallon Islands off the coast of San Francisco or Australia's Great Barrier Reef, it makes good sense to stay far away. Don't court trouble.

Navigation

For thousands of years, seafarers have found their way across trackless oceans on extended voyages of exploration and conquest. Lacking the technological aids at our disposal today, early Polynesians ventured thousands of miles from the Marquesas Islands to colonize Easter Island, and Mongol boaters braved the tempestuous Bering Sea to proliferate along the remote Aleutian archipelago and the western coast of North America. Vikings sailed and rowed across the stormy North Atlantic 1,000 years ago. The great Portuguese navigators and others sailed their way around the world by the stars. Intrepid modern-day explorers like Thor Heyerdahl and Ed Gillet have crossed the Atlantic and Pacific Oceans in native-style craft with a minimum of technical aids.

Navigation, the determination of where one is at sea and where one is going, is an essential skill for all kayakers intending to engage in kayaking expeditions and exploratory paddling. True, the availability of global positioning instruments (GPS), enabling paddlers to quickly pinpoint their location on the globe within a few meters, might seem to make a working knowledge of navigation principles unnecessary. But technology can, and often does, fail. The ability to use an old-fashioned compass effectively and to make sense of topographical maps and marine charts remains as important as ever for sea and coastal exploration.

Topographical maps are often more helpful than charts to sea kayakers because they depict beaches, mountains, and other land features that can help paddlers to navigate along a remote coastline, even though

Captain Jim Kakuk scans the horizon.

lights, buoys, and other marine navigational aids may not be present. It's also useful to fill the borders of maps and charts with information gathered about treacherous surf zones, tidal maelstroms, and other hazards, as well as references to interesting sea caves, wildlife colonies, freshwater, reefs where one can gather shellfish at low tide, and campsites. Yet, just as sea folk have always done, kayakers must ultimately rely on nature's cues for guidance.

Dead Reckoning

For sea kayakers, David Burch's *Fundamentals of Kayak Navigation* is gospel (see chapter 11, "Resources"). Burch teaches how to pilot and use dead reckoning. *Piloting* is simply referring to landmarks to guide you as you paddle along. For more precise piloting, it is useful to use a *range*, an alignment of two or more stationary objects. Derek Hutchinson calls this "navigation by transits." If you can line up the objects (say a sea stack and a mountaintop) and keep them lined up as you paddle toward them, you are assured of remaining on course. If the objects appear to move apart, you are paddling or drifting off course. Piloting using range is the coastal kayaker's basic navigational tool, effective wherever distinct rocks or land features are within sight. When range points are not indicated on your charts or clearly visible, a compass or GPS unit becomes useful.

Dead reckoning, useful in foggy conditions or when landmarks are otherwise not visible, involves considering cruising speed, time underway, and a compass course from a known point. Like piloting, it is *objective* navigation, that is, involving the use of charts, compasses, and mathematical calculations to determine present position and course to a destination. For accurate dead reckoning, use the stopwatch while paddling a known distance to determine your *mean speed* (speed plus or minus current and wind speed, taking into account weather conditions, boat load, rest periods, and other variables). Then calculate how long it will take to get to your destination by dividing the nautical miles of travel by your speed.

Though helpful at times, dead reckoning is not the only way to find your way around the marine environment.

> "The wind and the waves favor the ablest navigators."
>
> —Old seaman's saying

Many complex and interacting factors, such as swell action, longshore currents (which flow along the beach in the surf zone), rip currents (water flowing back to sea through channels after waves are spent), eddies (countercurrrents around obstacles), reflecting (bouncing) and refracting (bending) waves, lack of emergency escape routes, wind, fog and sea conditions, submerged or awash rocks, shoals, seasonal sandbars, channels through reefs, and inadequate charting of intercoastal zones combine to render it problematic at best. You may need to augment objective with subjective navigation to safely negotiate secret water paths among sea stacks and rock gardens.

Subjective Navigation

Instead of instruments and calculations, *subjective* navigation relies upon an internal metric inside your mind to calculate course and position. Just as the Polynesians memorized the movement of the heavens, how waves refracted around islands, the flight patterns of pelagic and shore seabirds, cloud patterns near land, and other subtle signs to guide them around the vast Pacific, we can learn the art of observing and responding to natural phenomena. With practice, this internal guidance system can become an amazingly effective method for getting around the coastal environment.

To navigate subjectively, one needs to gain proficiency at estimating the time of day, passage of time, distance traveled and distance to landmarks, and effect of wind, swells, and current upon boat speed and direction. Awareness of the effect of lunar cycles upon the tides and seasonal and latitudinal variations in the sky become as natural as remaining conscious of the speed limit on the freeway as one drives to work each day. If the battery in your watch expires suddenly, it's helpful to be able to look at the sun and know how much daylight remains before nightfall.

To learn subjective navigation, practice guessing how long five seconds is, using your watch for verification, until you get it right every time. Then progress to minutes and hours until you are guessing within a reasonable margin of error (say three minutes for an hour). Estimate how long it takes to perform routine activities and check against your clock. You will be surprised how your ability to judge time begins to improve.

Learn also to estimate speed and distance, using the car speedometer or known distances over which you travel as verifiers. Walking and paddling speeds are roughly the same (about three statute miles per hour), so remaining aware of time and distance while walking will improve your ability to guess your speed and distance on the water. Most of us have a sense of what 10 feet of length looks like. We know that a full stride equals about 3 feet and that a football field is 100 yards long. To gain familiarity with how a mile looks and feels, watch your car's odometer as you drive along. Better yet, get out in the natural environment as often as possible and be mindful of the relationship between time, pace, and distance traveled while walking or paddling over known distances.

Before beginning a paddle down an unfamiliar coastline, it's helpful to study your charts and topographic maps carefully and to commit as many significant factors to memory as possible. Identify key landmarks on the map and imagine what they might look like from the water. Once you are out in wind and big seas, attempting to read a chart from a wet and tippy kayak can be difficult. Be aware of the times and heights of high and low tides for the duration of your trip, and the speed and direction of tidal streams and currents. With experience, you will learn to plan your paddling itinerary to coincide with the ebb and flow of the tides. Tidal cycles and their corresponding currents increase in intensity during full and new moons and diminish during the neap.

There are many natural signs to guide an alert paddler through the marine environment. The sound of breaking surf on a fog-shrouded shoreline can reveal whether it is sand, cobbles, or cliffs. Subtle variations in water color provide clues about the character and depth of the sea bottom. Intact kelp beds indicate areas generally safe from breaking surf. Foam, circular riffles, and whirlpools on the surface are all indicators of interactions between currents and submerged rocks, shoals, or reefs. A hollow, echoing sound signals that sea caves are nearby. The pungent aroma of guano reveals the presence of bird or seal rookeries upwind.

Let Intuition Guide You

Except when venturing out in the open sea to frolic in a storm, extreme sea kayakers usually stick to the excitement zone near islands, reefs, or the mainland shore. Here charts are inadequate, compasses and other instruments generally go unheeded, mental calculations fall by the wayside, and intuition takes over.

Intuitive navigation entails making instant decisions about small, tactical direction changes based on a feeling. Here are some examples. As the sea draws out, you just *know* a big wave is coming, so you scoot behind a big rock and prepare for the wave when it comes. Or, you might feel your hackles rise for no discernible reason, and you *sense* a white shark is checking you out, so you leave the area. Or, a surfable wave is approaching, and you just intuitively *grok* where to set up for the best ride.

When entering a rock garden, sea cave, or other potentially explosive situation, a paddler must be poised to react instantaneously. In that moment, all the time and energy expended in practicing one's paddling skills and learning about the sea coalesce into reflexive action. It's an opportunity to allow the intuitive process full rein, and for the mind and body to work together to get you safely where you need to go.

In summary, use objective navigation to answer major questions, such as where are we now, where are we going today, and how long will it take to get there? Use subjective navigation to save time and augment your instruments by consciously reading the signs and making educated guesses. Finally, use intuitive navigation when on-the-scene information signals your mind and body to react to immediate environmental cues subconsciously.

A Subjective Navigation Scenario

A paddler, crossing a wide bay and using subjective navigation, might go through this thought process:

"Let's see . . . the sunrise was at 0600, and about 3 hours have elapsed since then, so it must be close to 0900—the tide is ebbing now, and the current should be ebbing in my favor. Yep, I see that kelp trailing seaward . . . once I cross this eddy fence, the main current will be behind me.

"I see from the riffles on the water's surface that the wind is about Force 2, but picking up. It's coming from the southwest, which means a tropical storm front could be moving in. So I'm paddling into the wind, but the 2-knot current is bumping up my 4-knot cruising speed a bit. That point looks like it's about 2 miles away. Those thunderheads on the horizon are probably still 15 miles out . . . but the wind's gonna be ripping in a half hour.

"That freighter coming into the bay from the west looks to be about a mile away, but I see by her bow wake that she's moving fast, maybe 10 knots, so I'll alter course to pass behind her. Those swells midchannel are probably 3 feet now, but they're on a collision course with that ebb current—which is due to increase to 4 knots within the next hour. Best to avoid that area! The waves are rolling in from the southwest, more evidence that a blow's coming. I'd better keep moving, or I could face some nasty conditions. The air and water temperatures both feel about 55°F, so I'm glad I'm wearing a wetsuit.

"I'm paddling perpendicular to the current and the wind, so I should make that pocket beach I spotted on the chart this morning in 20 minutes. Luckily, this bay is deep, probably 200 feet, so I shouldn't run into breaking waves until I get close to the point. If things are too crazy there I'll duck into an eddy behind that sea stack. Otherwise, I'll just let the current drag me around the point. If I can squeak through that rock garden on the lee side, it will be an easy sprint to the beach. That half-moon in the sky tells me the tides are moderate now, so I will probably not get swept away tonight. If I can maintain this pace, I'll make land and get my tent up before this storm hits."

The Dark Side of the Sea

Kayaking at night is not every paddler's idea of a good time. Add stormy conditions, and fewer still will heed the call. Pour this witch's brew upon the rocks, and only the most foolhardy show up. Yet, conditions may force you to paddle the coast at night. And for a few gonzo characters, paddling on the dark side is an exciting and mystical type of extreme sea kayaking. Pulling it off safely requires caution, special procedures and equipment, and an extra measure of good karma.

The Night Stuff

We listed equipment for night in chapter 2 (page 22). Use your waterproof flashlight for locating the other paddlers in your group, for signaling, and, in a limited sense, for finding your way. This should be tethered to your PFD or the deck of your kayak. Wear headlamps that leave the hands free to paddle and perform other essential functions. The problem with a personal light source is that it will illuminate the bow of your boat brilliantly, zapping your night vision and effectively leaving you even more isolated from the environment. If that's not bad enough, light attracts sharks. Additionally, excessive use of artificial light defeats the purpose of kayaking at night.

To be visible to one another, attach a chemical light stick to the back of your helmet. Stick reflective tape on your boat, PFD, helmet, and paddle if you plan to do a lot of night paddling, especially around harbors and shipping lanes where motor traffic might be a threat. A diver's compass on your wrist is easier to read in the gloom than a deck com-

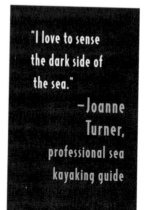

"I love to sense the dark side of the sea."

—Joanne Turner, professional sea kayaking guide

pass. Every night paddler should carry a set of aerial flares where they can be deployed quickly in an emergency.

Exploring the Exposed Coast at Night

Night time is not the right time to be exploring new and unfamiliar places. Darkness provides all the additional adventure you need without adding the potential danger of an unknown shoreline to the equation.

Of course, the optimum time for night paddling is when the sky is clear and a full moon is present. As you progress along a shoreline, pay special attention to landmarks, like a jagged promontory or other distinct land feature, so you can find your way back to camp. A useful habit that Michael learned as a boy when backpacking through the mountains of northern Idaho was to turn frequently and study the landscape (or seascape) from the reverse perspective. When paddling at night, take note also of the position of constellations and the moon in the sky, relative to the shoreline. This will be helpful in the unfortunate event that you wander away from visual contact with land. Remain alert for breaking waves or any disturbance on the water surface that might signify a shoal or barely submerged rocks.

Darkness and fog together make troublesome paddling companions! A few years ago, Jim Kakuk, Haruo Hasegawa, and Eric were paddling up an unexplored section of the rocky Oregon coast, looking for a safe campsite. At twilight, a wall of fog rolled in from the Pacific, making the search for a suitable campsite tenuous. The band groped along through the charcoal chowder until a hissing sound in the surf hinted that it might be breaking on sand instead of rock. A hurried powwow was held, and it was decided that Eric would surf in to shore and investigate. When Eric reemerged from the blackness a short time later, Haruo asked, "Eric, how did you find your way back to us?" Eric said that he "remembered" where his companions were waiting that night in the sea. It's encouraging to discover that the same intuitive homing process that guides migrating animals so well can be used by human beings in the fog at night.

How Difficult and Dangerous Is It?

In this chapter, we have discussed common elements to scout when kayaking—wind, weather, waves. In later chapters, we talk about scouting in specific instances, but for now, let's look at the basics of scouting and compare scouting and classification of rivers with oceans.

When scouting a river, kayakers will duck into an eddy or climb out and take a look at what lies ahead in the next set of rapids. They note hazards and lay out a route. What they see is what they get. River conditions remain constant during a short time period.

But the ocean changes quickly, all the time. You can scout from on the water or from on land. But what you see is not necessarily what you get, so scouting becomes more difficult. What is needed is a way to classify general danger, so a person knows whether it's too extreme to kayak that day.

River Difficulty System

River runners have devised an international classification system to rate the difficulty and danger of a river section or rapid. It goes like this: *Class 1* is moving water with only a few riffles, waves, and obstructions. *Class 2* has small rapids, waves up to 3 feet, and wide and clear channels with some maneuvering needed. *Class 3* has rapids with high, irregular waves and narrow passages with complex maneuvering. *Class 4* is long and difficult rapids with constricted passages requiring precise maneuvering and Eskimo rolls and with dangerous conditions that make rescue difficult. *Class 5* is extremely long, difficult, and very violent rapids that require very precise techniques, and loss of life is possible in a mishap. *Class 6* is Class 5 taken to an extreme; nearly impossible conditions are suitable for a team of experts only, and loss of life is probable in a mishap.

The rating system is subjective, but it is an indicator of what a boater should anticipate. For example, if you don't have a reliable roll, you should stay out of water rated Class 3 or above. Also, a river's rating may go up in the winter when it's cold outside or if the river flow increases.

An Ocean Classification System

Whereas a river's difficulty level is based on flow and gradient, the ocean's is based on wind and waves, which change all the time. Thus, devising a classification system to help boaters choose when to go out in a particular sea on a given day is more imprecise and complex than on the river. Many factors need to be considered. We have developed a system that may be useful for sea kayakers in rating their paddling area.

Each of the 10 factors has been weighted depending upon its difficulty or danger. Factor 1, *water temperature*, starts at 72° F because that is a temperature at which most people can swim comfortably, and it happens to be 40° F above freezing. As noted earlier, cold water is the number one killer of kayakers, so it receives a lot of weight in the algorithm. To calculate factor 1, subtract the actual water temperature from 72 and list the remainder as the score. Actual water temperature is superior to an imprecise, statement such as "That's some cold water!"

Factor 2, *wind speed*, is similar to flow rate in rivers. The more wind, the more difficult and dangerous the conditions become. Wind is also fickle; it may increase or decrease at a moment's notice. That's why we give it so many potential points. Calculation of wind speed score is simple; the score is the same as the observed or estimated high mean wind speed in the windiest time and place you may paddle. Wind speed in statute mph is a better indicator than generalizations that are not measurable, such as "The wind is blowing really hard, mate."

Wave height, factor 3, like wind speed, is measured in actual vertical feet. All you have to do is watch the waves and then estimate the high mean vertical wave height. Wave height is measured separately from whether the wave is breaking (factor 5). The height of the wave *face* is not part of this calculation. The actual wave height in feet is used because this is much more valid a measurement than a person's subjective feeling: "The waves are, like, totally huge, man." To calculate, estimate the mean high wave size in feet and multiply by 2 to obtain the weighted wave height score.

Factor 4 is the "how long can you tread water?" variable. It represents an estimate of *how far you would have to* swim to reach safety should you lose your boat. Each interval of 100 meters is represented by 1 point up to 2,000 meters or more, over a mile, at which point you would be better off awaiting rescue (20 points). Note that the first four factors are *always* calculated in any sea kayaking endeavor, even in a protected harbor.

Factor 5 is the *surf zone*. If waves over 2 feet are *breaking*, add 30 points. We give factor 5 a lot of weight because waves become much more powerful when they break on the sea floor. If special circumstances are operating in the surf zone, add more points when you compute factor 10, miscellaneous conditions.

Factor 6 is a *rock garden*. If you go into it, add 20 points. Do the same for factor 7, a *sea cave*. If waves are breaking onto a rock garden and you go through it to get into a sea cave, add 30 + 20 + 20 to get a combined factor of 70; divide by 20 to obtain 3.5 (Class 3)—and that's before you add in the first four required factors!

Factors 8 and 9, *night* and *dense fog* conditions, each rate an automatic 20 points (one class increase). As with factors 5 through 7, if they appear together, add 40 points to your total, which increases the risk two whole classes.

Factor 10 is a hodgepodge category to score 10 or more points for *unusual, temporary,* or *local hazards* such as ship traffic or sleet. For example, an area noted for tidal streams, icebergs, or shark attacks would receive an extra 10 points. Or if a wave face at a beach is nearly vertical and dumping or features a very strong rip current, add 10 points as a miscellaneous factor.

Sea Conditions Rating System (SCRS)

Factor	Computation Method	Maximum Points	Score
1. Water temperature	1 point for each degree below 72°F	40	_____
2. Wind speed	1 point per mph of wind speed	50+	_____
3. Wave height	2 points per vertical wave foot	40+	_____
4. Swim distance	1 point per 100 meters	20	_____
5. Surf zone	30 points if waves are breaking	30	_____
6. Rock garden	20 points if rocks are present	20	_____
7. Sea cave	20 points if entering sea caves	20	_____
8. Night	20 points if it is night	20	_____
9. Fog	up to 20 points if fog is dense	20	_____
10. Miscellaneous	10 points or more for danger	10+	_____
		TOTAL POINTS	_____
	Divide total points by 20 to obtain CLASS LEVEL		_____

Scoring Directions: Scope out the sea using conservative estimates or instruments, and give scores to each factor. Add scores and place sum in the space next to "TOTAL POINTS." Divide the sum by 20 to convert to the "CLASS LEVEL":

Class 1 *(score up to 1.9)—easy to moderate difficulty, danger, and skills required*

Class 2 *(score from 2.0 to 2.9)—intermediate difficulty, danger, and skills required*

Class 3 *(3.0 to 3.9)—advanced difficulty, danger, and skills (e.g., a reliable roll and self-rescue a must)*

Class 4 *(4.0 to 4.9)—extreme conditions, advanced techniques required, loss of life possible*

Class 5 *(5.0 to 5.9)—very extreme, life-threatening conditions*

Class 6 *(6.0+)—nearly impossible conditions, suitable only for a team of experts, loss of life probable in a mishap*

Sample Situations Using the SCRS

Here are typical examples for each class. For Class I, say Princeton Harbor in the summer, the water temperature is 52°F (20 points), wind speed is 9 mph (9 points), wave height is I foot (2 points), swim distance to safety is 400 meters (4 points), and there are no other factors. Points total 35, divided by 20 = 1.75. Just about any kayaker wearing proper clothes who can swim can safely paddle here. If we add dense fog (20 points) to this equation, we'd total 55, divided by 20 = 2.75. Now it's Class 2+, still doable but more dangerous. You can see that even a small, protected harbor on a calm day may rate higher than Class I.

If you wanted to kayak surf at a break such as Montara Beach, you would calculate the difficulty like this. Water temperature is 52°F (20 points), wind speed is 8 mph (8), wave height is 5 feet (10), maximum swimming distance to safety is 200 meters (2), and you are in a surf zone (30). Your point total is 70, divided by 20 = 3.5, so it's Class 3. At this class, you know you are paddling in rough conditions and must have a good roll and rescue skills. If there were local factors operating, such as an exceptionally steep beach break, you might add 10 or more points and recompute your score. For more on surf zones, read chapter 5.

Let's say you wanted to play in the rock garden just south of Montara Beach on the same day. You add 20 points because of the rock garden (everything else remains the same) and achieve a new total score of 90, divided by 20 = 4.5—Class 4. This is extreme sea kayaking and requires intuitive navigation and advanced paddling skills. This is best attempted with a competent team, never alone (see chapter 7).

Perhaps you wanted to explore the nearby Montara sea cave in the same conditions. You are still in 5-foot surf and rocks. The cave adds yet another 20 points for a total of 110, divided by 20 = 5.5—Class 5. This cave, in these conditions, should only be explored by a team of experts, because even though the waves aren't that high, they compress in caves, and you could be entrapped or smashed. Chapter 8 describes caving features and technique.

Needless to say, Class 5 should not be attempted unless you and your team of experts are prepared for possible death. What constitutes a Class 6 in sea kayaking? Let's say you want to go storm kayaking, and are leaving from Princeton Harbor into the open sea. The water temperature is still 52°F (20 points), the wind is now 40 mph (40 points), the waves at sea are 20 feet high (40), and you are two miles offshore (20). Your score is 120 points, divided by 20 = 6—Class 6. Sound dangerous? It is. In chapter 6 we discuss how to kayak in storm seas.

What does a Class 6 surf zone look like? Let's say you were the world's greatest surf kayaker and wanted to try your luck at the infamous Mavericks Break in the winter in perfect conditions. Let's scout it out, factor by factor. Factor 1, water temperature, is still 52°F (20 points). Factor 2, wind speed, is negligible (0). Factor 3, vertical wave height, is 20 feet (40). Factor 4, swim distance to safety, is 1,000 meters (10). Factor 5, breaking surf, is happening (30). Factor 6, rocks, is added in because the break occurs at Pillar Point, and you could easily be swept into the rocks while broaching after your ride (20). Factors 7, 8, and 9 are not applicable. The miscellaneous category of factor 10 is considered because the wave face is steep, and the wave crest pitches violently off the top when it breaks (10 points). We add the factor scores together for a total of 130, divided by 20 = 6.5 (Class 6+). Voilà—one of the world's most dangerous surf breaks on an ideal day!

Photocopy the Sea Conditions Rating System (SCRS) from this book and use it to compute the risk factors each time you go sea kayaking. Have everyone in your party compute their estimates, and then compare. If scores differ, discuss them with your teammates. Use your SCRS to help you gauge and improve your scouting and rating abilities. Use instruments, weather reports, and your subjective navigational estimates in concert to assign points to each factor.

Don't underestimate conditions in order to appear macho or to sucker people into doing activities beyond their skills. The SCRS is just a general guideline, an indicator; it doesn't account for freak incidents such as williwaws, waterspouts, and tsunamis. Remember that sea state changes *rapidly*, so don't be lulled into a week-long paddle in Class 4 conditions because the SCRS indicator was only Class 2 when you set out. Be conservative and assign points based on the worst conditions you are likely to face. One final consideration: the SCRS only rates sea conditions, not the suitability of your equipment, or your mental or physical preparation, or the skill levels of each person in your party.

Now that you have read these first four chapters, you have an inkling of what extreme sea kayaking is all about, know the necessary equipment and basic skills, and are aware of common elements that comprise the mighty sea. The following four chapters describe what to do in the surf (chapter 5), along the exposed coast and open sea (chapter 6), among rocks (chapter 7), and inside sea caves (chapter 8). Let's go!

Cold water and 5-foot breaking surf in a rock garden south of Point Montara add up to Class 4 conditions.

The Surf Zone

> From the bluff, the waves looked inviting. But from the beach, they were terrifying.
>
> —Nancy Soares, sportswoman

It's understandable that surf zones are respected, even feared, by many ocean kayakers. Yet most sea kayakers who venture along exposed coasts will eventually have to face paddling in and out through breaking surf. Kayak surfing is also excellent preparation for rock and cave exploration and paddling in extreme weather conditions. Some especially adventuresome kayakers, like mountaineers who prefer extreme technical climbing to trekking, deliberately seek out the surf and rarely bother with touring on flat water. In contrast, paddlers who never perfect their surf zone skills will lack confidence when faced with launching and landing through breaking waves and rock gardens. This will limit the places they can explore on exposed wilderness coasts.

Misha Dynnikov accelerates down the face of a winter wave in La Push, Washington.

The Perfect Surfing Wave

Any water where waves are breaking is sure to provide excitement and challenge for paddlers. But some waves are much better to surf than others. Just for fun, let's envision the optimal conditions for kayak surfing. We're standing on a pristine beach, gazing out over the exposed sea and preparing to launch our kayaks and surf the waves. It's a sunny day, and the air temperature is a balmy 80°F. The heat building up under our wetsuits makes us eager to get wet. We step into the water and allow it to swirl around our feet. It's

Why Do They Call It *Mavericks?*

The infamous surf break called Mavericks, on the northern California coast, is regarded as an ultimate rite of passage for fearless big-wave surfers from all over the world. It lies just off Pillar Point, near the little town of Half Moon Bay. It got its name from a dog who used to accompany one of the early board surfers there. But the gargantuan waves that develop on this point in winter are truly mavericks themselves. They seem to come out of nowhere and break with tremendous force; then they crash over a rock garden covered with razor sharp mussels. Long feared and revered by locals, Mavericks's reputation grew even more ominous when Hawaiian big-wave surfer Mark Foo challenged it and died one December day in 1994.

Nearly a decade before that tragic occurrence, I moved to the coast and met Michael. Eager to explore every inch of this dramatic coastline, I was ecstatic the day we first paddled out to Pillar Point reef in our kayaks. The inside break where Michael led me was relatively safe in comparison to Mavericks, which lay on the exposed, outer edge of the reef system, a few hundred feet to the north. Even though we could plainly see Mavericks breaking from where we surfed, I still had no sense of just how big and powerful it was. But the time would soon come when I would find out.

One stormy morning a few days later, I led fellow Ranger Glenn Gilchrist on a 3-hour tour of the local sights. We launched at Moss Beach and approached Pillar Point from the north about a half-hour later. As we drew near the reef, I warned Glenn to keep a sharp eye out for the huge Mavericks waves, which could rise up suddenly and break, far to seaward. No sooner had this warning left my lips than a massive comber materialized outside, bearing straight for us. I could feel my heart pounding as Glenn and I spun our boats around to face this El Capitan of the sea. We barely managed to claw our way over the cornice of that first towering wave, only to be confronted by another, even bigger wave building up outside. Once again we flailed at the water, our arms burning, until we punched through the wave just as it was beginning to break. We gasped for air and laughed with relief at our close call.

But bad news often comes in threes, and this was no exception. The biggest, baddest, boldest Bagwan of them all, as high as a three-story apartment building, reared up and bared its fangs. I lowered my head and paddled with all my strength as the wave steepened in front of me. A dozen feet or more of the wave's crest spilled over me, filling my ears with the hiss of trapped air from the whirlwind inside. I felt myself being sucked deeper into its maw, as megatons of energy started tumbling down. In the midst of all the chaos, I glimpsed a lime-colored wall of solid water near the crest of the wave and drove my bow toward it with everything I had. Bursting through, I sailed three fathoms down the back of that brute and splashed down in open water.

My own ordeal over, I stared back into Mavericks, looking for my partner. "Oh no," I thought, "Glenn's still trapped in there somewhere." But then I spotted him, out in relatively calm water beyond the break zone. By some miracle, he had also escaped.

(continued on page 55)

refreshing enough to warrant wearing neoprene but presents no threat of hypothermia.

Sunset pastels will soon begin to fill the heavens, and shafts of golden light are shining down. A double rainbow arches above dark storm clouds in the western sky. The light offshore breeze helps to steepen the waves and blows a little spindrift off their tops. A sweet blend of spilling and plunging waves, with well-defined shoulders breaking both left and right, beckons us. In these ideal conditions, it will be possible for more than one paddler to safely surf out there. The faces are smooth, not too choppy or steep, evidence that these swells were generated by a distant storm and not by nearby winds. The waves range from about 5 feet high (big enough to provide a fun ride) to just below life threatening (for real excitement). Outgoing rip channels flow out at either side of the break, making it easy to dash back outside to the takeoff zone. We envision ourselves making it through the breakers, reaching the optimal setup zone, taking off smoothly, and getting great rides.

Yet, in the surf, conditions are rarely this inviting. It's always worthwhile to observe the ocean for a while before paddling into it, either from shore or from a kayak out in deep water that is not breaking. If the surf seems at or above your skill level, take a few moments to complete the SCRS sheet. At an especially hazardous location, like an exposed point or the mouth of a river, where strong currents are interacting with oncoming surf, it becomes very important to study the situation carefully before paddling into the breaking water. Oncoming swells, especially in combination with a strong flooding tide, can roll upstream and collide with the flow of a river, creating

Misha Dynnikov surfs
a near-perfect wave.

(continued from page 54)

Later he would confess to me that when he looked up and saw the crest curling over, he thought he was done for. But that capricious wave had apparently expended most of its force over me, and it tossed Glenn aside like a sumo wrestler heaving a hobbit out of the ring. We were both so grateful not to have been driven onto the rocks by those waves that we crossed ourselves and offered thanks to Neptune. Once again, we had been allowed to pass through the battleground where land and sea wage eternal war, without receiving a scratch. We learned that it pays to observe the waves—from a safe perch!

—Eric

Jim Kakuk breaks the wave
barrier by punching through
the surf with his paddle and
torso thrust forward.

chaotic areas filled with immense standing waves. If you see any surf that looks too big and steep, is torn up by the wind or dumping violently, or could drive an out-of-control boater into the rocks, it may be wise to move on to a kinder, gentler place. Even in the best of times, a surf zone is a place where powerful forces are at work. When conditions get extreme, you could easily lose your boat or get hurt. Always look long and hard before you leap in.

Ins and Outs of the Surf Zone

Not every sea kayaker deliberately chooses to play in surf. But, as expedition paddler Valerie Fons discovered, most folks who paddle open coasts end up, sooner or later, having to fight through breakers. At such times, surf skills and experience are great to have. Let's explore how to launch out through surf from shore and, perhaps even more important, how to get back in through it to make a safe landing.

Getting Out through Surf

Before paddling out into and through a surf zone, take the time to observe it carefully from the beach. Check over your boat and make sure all loose gear is secured. Are both your fore and aft float bags fully inflated and all hatches buttoned down tightly? Are you wearing a proper wetsuit and other protective clothing for a protracted swim in these conditions? Finally, do some stretches, check the buckles on your helmet and life vest, and jump into the sea to acclimate to the water and get warmed up.

If you're paddling a closed-cockpit boat, carry or drag it to the shiny wet sand at the water's edge and align the bow with the oncoming surf. Slip into your cockpit, secure your sprayskirt, and push back against the sand with your paddle on one side and your free hand on the other, propelling yourself toward the water until a wave lifts you up. You're off!

If your craft is an open-cockpit (sit-on-top) design, grab hold of the bow toggle or forward side rail and pull the boat behind or to the side of you as you stride into the water. When knee deep in surge, move your boat forward to bring the cockpit alongside where you stand, slide your hips into position in the seat, and then swing your feet onboard and into place. Never try to step across and straddle your boat before sitting down, for if a wave crashes into the boat while you are standing over it, you will do the splits and be sent sprawling.

Whether in an open- or closed-cockpit boat, ensure that your boat is still pointing straight out, perpendicular to the oncoming waves. If it's not, execute a few quick sweep strokes to swing your bow back to where the waves are hitting it straight on. Look at the surf ahead—it's amazing how much higher the waves look now than when you were standing on the beach. Remember to take a few deep breaths and relax. Fasten your seat belt if you have one and check that your hands loosely grip the paddle shaft about shoulder width apart. Then, stroke on with gusto.

Unless the shorebreak is very steep, there's no need to rush out into deeper water. The shallow water near shore, called the *soup zone*, is a good place to practice maneuvers

and get further tuned in. There will be plenty of time to paddle out and engage the big breakers. If you run into problems here, you should be able to make it back to the beach easily. But be warned that capsizing or pitch-poling a kayak in shallow water can cause your head or shoulder to hit the sand, so lean deeply into waves in a low brace and make your hull impact the sand first.

A combination of power, sweep, and back strokes should enable you to maintain your position in the surging water near shore. Each time an oncoming wave lifts the bow of your boat and starts to drive you backward, lean forward and execute a few powerful forward strokes. Between waves, practice an Eskimo roll or two. When a wave rolls in from the side, use your paddle and the weight of your upper torso to low brace solidly into it. This useful technique, called *broaching*, enables you to remain upright when being driven sideways by balancing your own weight and power against the energy of the wave. By bracing deeply into a wave while broaching, the hull of your boat (rather than your head and upper torso) is positioned forward as you move along, a buffer between you and the sand.

Making the Big Move

After warming up in the foam at the surf's inner edge, focus on the outer breakers and envision yourself paddling through those waves and reaching the calm area beyond. Watch for a window of opportunity, a relatively calm period that *sometimes* comes after the last breaking wave of a set. Through experience, you'll learn how to recognize these windows and go for it.

When you sense a window has arrived, paddle hard, straight out to sea. Look for *green zones*, sections of waves whose crests have not begun to topple and break. Steve Sinclair called zigging from green zone to green zone through the surf *establishing trajectories*. Recognizing and seeking out green zones diminishes your chances of getting driven back by breaking waves.

Don't worry when a green zone you are heading toward disappears and a wave suddenly breaks ahead of you. Just vector toward the weakest looking section of the white, boiling foam that appears after a wave has broken.

Wait for the initial power of the foaming break to subside (even back-paddle if necessary). Then, just before the wave reaches you, resume power stroking ahead forcefully, thrusting your paddle and upper body forward just before impact. Continue your progress in this way, seeking out a series of green and white zones until you've made it through the breaking surf.

Five Not-So-Easy Choices

Sooner or later, you'll look up into the face of the invincible wave, a monster so big, so scary, you think you're doomed. What can you do? You actually have five choices, so use intuitive navigation to take in relevant information quickly and act decisively. Each choice has its good and bad points.

Your first choice is to take a deep breath, relax everything except your grip on your paddle, and surrender to the flow. Sometimes this works, but we advise against it. By relinquishing personal control and doing nothing, you may increase your chances of being injured or having your boat damaged.

Another option is to turn upside down, bail out of your kayak, and dive toward the bottom, like a seal. This technique works best if you are paddling an open-deck boat. Once the wave thunders over you and you pop back up on the surface, you may be some distance from your boat and paddle. Retrieve these on your swim back to the beach. There you may face the additional insult of being referred to by your paddling companions as a "squirmin' hatch blower." Actually, there is nothing dishonorable about ditching your boat to escape a beating. The sailor's maxim of "sticking with your boat" doesn't apply here, unless you intend to go down with the ship. The bail-out-and-dive technique is best reserved for only the most extreme circumstances.

A third choice is recommended by Derek Hutchinson, who suggests that when you come face to face with an intimidating comber, roll over and allow it to crash down upon your boat's upturned bottom. When the turbulence eases, just roll back up. The advantage of this maneuver is that the force of the breaking wave is absorbed by your hull rather than your head and upper body. The drawback

of this rollover method is that it doesn't work so well in plunging waves over 8 feet, where your boat might get sucked into the curl and be hurled end over end, with you hanging powerless and exposed underneath.

The fourth choice works best when paddling a highly maneuverable craft like a wave ski or surf shoe, or a squirt, slalom, or surf kayak, or a small open-cockpit play boat such as the Tsunami X-7 Mojo. Before the wave reaches you, spin your boat around 180 degrees and face the shore. As soon as you feel the big breaker lifting the tail of your kayak into the sky, do a quick power stroke, lean forward, and prepare to go ballistic. As you accelerate down the face, shift your weight or steer with your rudder and paddle blade to turn left or right, as the wave dictates. With luck, you can surf it all the way to shore. This method doesn't work well with a longer boat that is slower to turn around. Chances are you may get caught sideways by tons of water crashing down upon you.

The final choice is simply to muster all your strength, race straight toward the wave, and punch over the top of it. If the wave is cresting high

Punching through a breaking wave.

above your head, redouble your paddling efforts and pierce the weakest looking spot. Amazingly, some breakers seem to hesitate at this last moment before plunging downward, giving the committed paddler a chance to claw over or through the lip of the curling wave and *break the wave barrier*. If you fail to make it over the top of the wave, you will then fall *backward* down its face. At this point, either hang in until you regain control, or exercise option number two: bail out and dive toward the bottom. Of the five choices, we usually opt for this last one because you save a lot of time and energy if you just clear the wave and get through the surf zone.

Coming in through the Surf

Once you've made it past the breakers and into the open sea beyond, you well deserve this opportunity to relax, celebrate, and enjoy the ocean. Eventually, you will have to get back in. Your journey back in through the surf zone demands many of the same skills executed on the way out, only now you're going *with* the wave's power, rather than opposing it.

Once again, watch the waves carefully as you edge closer to the breaking surf, and look out for rocks, people, or other hazards. Keeping the stern of your boat pointed straight out to sea should enable you to back-paddle over any rolling waves that build up behind you. When the surf is small, the consequences of poor timing or judgment are usually not serious. But when the waves grow huge and gnarly, paddling in among those moving mountains becomes a daunting affair. Once again, different strategies can be selected for paddling in through a surf zone.

Three Ways Home

The usual plan is to wait for a pause between big waves and then to paddle at top speed to reach shore. You want to reach the beach, or at least protected water, before a large wave overtakes you. This option works well when seas are relatively calm and wave sets are arriving in a somewhat predictable pattern.

However, when waves are big and being generated by a nearby storm, with brief or unpredictable windows between them, the chances of making it in without getting clobbered grow slim. Under these circumstances, it's sometimes wise to wait for the last wave in a medium-sized set, paddle just hard enough to catch a ride on the lip of a wave without dropping down onto its actual face, and let the forward momentum carry you as far as possible toward shore. When the wave begins to break, back-paddle off the lip so the wave breaks in *front* of you. Then stroke hard through the foam, follow the breaking wave toward shore, and try to make it in before another large wave comes charging in behind you.

Your final choice of strategies for making it in through the breakers is the one guaranteed to generate the most enthusiasm among the hodads watching from shore, and also the one that requires the most skill—surfing a big wave in. This is a risky procedure unless executed properly, but it is definitely the fastest and most exciting way to the beach. Carefully select the most surfable looking wave, with shoulders that break gradually on the sides, not dumping all at once.

To launch onto a wave, lean forward and take a few strokes with your paddle, feel the stern of your craft rise as the wave builds behind you—and in a jiffy you are rocketing along with all that power. Now it becomes important to exercise some control over your position on the wave. If the breaker grows steep and you shoot too far down the face, the bow of your boat will *pearl* (plunge deep into the water ahead), causing you to cartwheel or *endo* (flip over). This looks spectacular, but it puts tremendous stress on a fully laden sea kayak and can even cause it to break up amidships. To reduce this possibility, lean back, which slows your progress on the wave, and rudder or pivot to turn the kayak whichever way seems most appropriate on the wave.

If you end up sideways in a broach, immediately throw your weight and your paddle blade into the oncoming wave and perform a *low brace*: keep your wrists straight (not extended) and your elbows bent and locked in close to your body (not

Jim Kakuk does a pirouette.

Alan Hillesheim

straight and away from your body) to absorb the shock and avoid shoulder dislocation. If this is done right, you will bounce along, somewhat upright, until the energy of the wave plays out. By then you should be close to shore.

The main disadvantage of broaching is that you have little or no control over where you are going, and conceivably you could collide with rocks, other kayakers, or swimmers who happen to be in front of you. For this reason, it's important to locate a clear path before heading in through the surf.

Surf-Zone Etiquette

Speaking of broaching, it's time to consider surf-zone safety and etiquette. Courtesy in the surf zone is extremely important, not just for social reasons, but also to reduce the chances of kayakers colliding with each other and other water-sports enthusiasts who may happen to be out in the surf zone.

Unfortunately, many board surfers have grown antagonistic toward kayakers. This is due, in part, to the fact that an out-of-control kayak in a surf zone is a big, heavy, and fast-moving projectile, kind of like a bulldozer moving across a prairie dog colony. Inexperienced and "expert" kayakers continue to blunder into surf spots and cause chaos. So if you want to kayak surf and are not experienced, it's best to first seek out uncrowded waters.

The Banzai Bozos, a team of seasoned kayak surfers from the Sonoma coast, once paddled out to Steamers Lane at Santa Cruz, a surf spot occupied by a territorial enclave of board surfers. The board surfers were predictably hostile, an altercation ensued, and one of the Bozos ended up smacking one of the board surfers. A few months later, another kayaker, Tom Monaghan, was physically attacked by board surfers while out in the water at Steamers.

Many board surfers are courteous, but enough are territorial to warrant finding surf zones far from the madding crowd of board surfers. So leave the urban beaches to swimmers, jet skiers, and board surfers, and seek out remote, hard-to-reach point and reef breaks.

Courtesies While Paddling Out

To stay out of the way of another kayaker who may be surfing or broaching in on a wave, always paddle out on the edge and not up the middle of a surfing area. Take advantage of rip currents if possible.

Avoid spearing people in the surf.

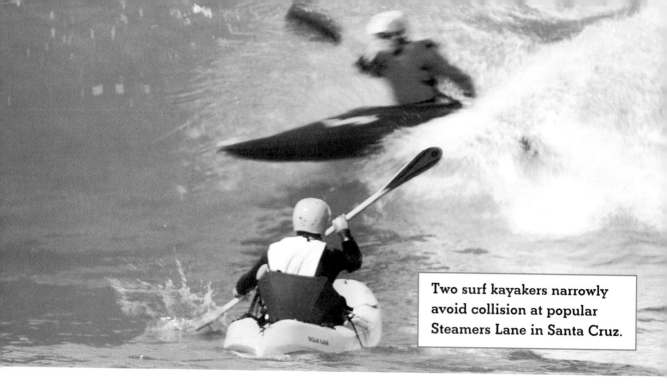

Don't bunch up with other paddlers or allow a column to form, with boats stacked up one behind the other. It's best to fan out and leave plenty of room between yourself and the others, in case a big wave comes in and starts hurtling boats backward.

If you spot a kayaker *surfing* toward you, simply move away from the surfer's intended route. Look for a green zone that you can reach before the breaking wave and the surfer reach you. It is the responsibility of outgoing paddlers to notice and move out of the way of incoming surfers, who are moving much faster and may have limited visibility.

A paddler *broaching* toward you on a wave has very little control over the boat's direction and an obscured view of what is ahead. So quickly vector left or right to get as far out of the way as possible. It is completely up to *you*, as the outgoing paddler, to avoid a collision.

Should a broaching boat be moments from hitting you, point your bow away from the broacher. Once you are as parallel as possible to the oncoming boat, at the last second brace and lean away from the broacher and toward shore. This will place your hull between you and the oncoming boat like a shield. You will probably end up being capsized, but at least you have avoided exposing your upper body to impact. Don't automatically roll upside down as a broacher

approaches because you can no longer see what is happening and risk getting struck while upside down.

If two boats do collide solidly, the paddlers should head for shore and check for damage. If either kayaker appears to be injured, remain calm and assess the situation. If anyone involved has become disabled and is unable to paddle, the other may elect to tow the injured paddler and boat to safety. If an injured paddler is out of the boat and in the water, encourage the paddler to grab hold of the boat from the seaward side and to face toward shore. If you are injured and alone, sit or recline low in your boat and allow the wind and the waves to push you toward shore. If you are injured and lose your boat, swim in to shore as quickly as you can muster, before shock sets in. Signal for help by waving a paddle or arm wildly above your head and whistling or shouting. In any case, able paddlers should remain close by injured companions until everyone has reached shore safely.

Courtesy When Surfing

To avoid accidents, always observe surf etiquette. Here are some basic rules to follow when kayak surfing:

- *Make sure the way is clear ahead before taking off on a wave.*

- Respect the right-of-way of the paddler closest to the break, in what's called the sweet spot.
- Yield to anyone who gets on a wave before you do.
- Back off the wave if someone else drops in near you, even if you have the right-of-way.
- Quickly cut away if someone is surfing alongside you on a wave.
- Never surf backward unless you're sure no one is downwave from you.
- Never surf directly toward someone.
- Don't attempt to share a wave with other kayakers or board surfers, unless there's lots of room and everyone can stay far apart for the whole ride.
- Be considerate and take turns.
- Move over to the side of the break after your ride and stay out of the way of others as you paddle back out.
- Be quick to respond if anyone capsizes, becomes separated from his or her boat, or otherwise gets in trouble.

Always strive to remain in control while riding a wave. If you must go into a broach to avoid capsizing, remain alert for any UFO (unidentified floating object) that may be in your path. Even while broaching, you can use your paddle to move your boat laterally on the wave to avoid contact with exposed rocks, a floating object, or another kayaker. If you spot anything ahead of you while broaching, dig your paddle deeper into the wave behind you. This may slow your mo-

A Surf Zone Calamity

In 1986, Jim Kakuk and I were teaching a surf-zone skills class at north Stinson Beach. A few dozen kayakers practicing for a surfing contest joined us in the water. The waves were only about 2 to 3 feet high, but the surf kayakers were unsafe maniacs and followed no safety protocol. We realized the surf was too crowded and dangerous for us, so we rounded up our students and sent them to shore. Then disaster struck.

A woman was sitting at the bottom of the surf route, spellbound by her boyfriend, who was half surfing, half broaching on a little mush wave. Somehow, he managed to spear the woman in the back with the bow of his slalom kayak. She immediately slumped forward in her cockpit. An alert kayaker and I quickly paddled to each side of her, propping her up. She was already in deep shock, and her life force ebbed with the tide. Another paddler hailed a passing fishing boat just outside the surf. The fisherman called an air ambulance on his VHF radio, while we managed to escort her to the side of the fishing boat.

The victim needed to get out of the water soon, so we carefully hauled her and the kayak out of the water and onto the deck of the fishing boat. Once on board, the two good Samaritan kayakers and I gently pulled her out of the cockpit, while supporting her head, neck, and back. She was placed on her back, stabilized, and treated for shock. As we comforted her, I remarked, "We need a doctor here."

Her boyfriend, staring guiltily at her and wringing his hands, popped out of his self-pitying stupor and said, "I'm a doctor."

"Well, then, get over here and do something," I commanded. He obeyed and took over. I jumped overboard and paddled my kayak to shore, just as the helicopter landed. As the gawking horde surrounded the victim, I split the scene.

We later learned that she recovered from the punctured lung she suffered in the collision. Lessons learned? A near-fatal collision can occur easily in the smallest surf, so pay attention and follow surf etiquette. Know first aid and assist those who need help. Never space out in self-reproach.

—Eric

mentum and will rotate the hull of your boat up and out in front of you. Thus, your hull and the water cushion it pushes ahead will stay between your upper torso and anything with which you may collide. Be careful not to brace so far back that you capsize completely, as this also will place you at risk when hurtling over a barely submerged reef.

where the waves are building up height and steepness but are not yet breaking. Point the bow of your kayak toward shore but glance around to keep your eye on the swells building up behind you. When you see a wave approaching that looks surfable, start paddling to build up forward speed. Though facing forward, you'll know when the wave

Beth Borgeson braces to keep control while broaching in the surf.

Kayak Surfing

Surfing a kayak down a wave is a thrilling experience, but like any other high-speed, high-adrenaline activity, it can be perilous for the inexperienced. It's best to seek out the company of a seasoned group or paddling instructor and to learn in stages. Stick at first to smaller waves and uncrowded surf zones, free of strong currents and rock or coral hazards. As your experience and ability grow, you will be able to graduate safely to bigger and more challenging surf. Continue to paddle with skilled companions, since it's safer and more fun than going out alone.

To surf a wave, paddle to the section of a surf zone

arrives because the stern of your kayak will lift up, and you will feel yourself accelerating. Now things begin to happen fast, where experience and practice start to make a big difference. The object is to remain on the moving wave, in that *pocket* located just forward of the break. To accomplish this, you may have to make a succession of subtle but rapid adjustments, shifting your body weight or ruddering to turn, leaning back to put the brakes on, or leaning forward in combination with a few power strokes to shoot ahead on the wave. When the wave begins to play out, cut out of your wave and immediately paddle to the edge of the break to avoid incoming surf (and any others who may be riding it). Then, paddle back out to the setup spot.

Surf Frolic

Like board surfers, kayakers can do all kinds of tricks on the waves. Just what you should attempt

John Lull and Eric Soares maintain a safe distance apart while riding a wave.

depends on your experience, the general surf conditions, and the kind of boat you are paddling. Long, sleek sea kayaks are best for covering long distances and can deliver fast, smooth rides on big, rolling, deep-water waves. Shorter slalom or squirt river boats have less hull speed but turn quicker and are more maneuverable and easier to roll, definite advantages in breaking waves or around rocks. Kayak surfers continually discover new ways to use their boats in breaking water. Someday, kayak teams may perform choreographed surfing maneuvers in a veritable surf circus.

One common stunt maneuver is the *loop*, or endo, where the bow or stern of the kayak is intentionally allowed to submarine beneath the surface at the leading edge of a wave. To initiate a forward loop, bend your upper torso forward over your knees as you drop down a steep wave face. The resultant weight shift will cause you to shoot ahead until the bow plunges into the water at the bottom of the wave. In that moment when your boat is standing vertical and practically free from water friction, an energetic hip snap can cause it to spin 360 degrees or more, in a pirouetting motion. Or you can continue to pitch forward and complete your loop. Try spinning just enough as you fall forward to land on the boat's hull, rather than on your face. Then, with a sweep of your paddle, snap back up and resume surfing, backwards now, on the wave. These are beautiful maneuvers to watch when executed properly.

Endless variations on endos, loops, and turns become within reach as your skills evolve, so feel free to experiment and grow. Derek Hutchinson tells of a surf kayaker in a competition who once surfed down a wave, pirouetted, looped, and did an Eskimo roll—all without a paddle. Nice trick!

Conceivably, a surf master on a well-formed wave could roller-coaster down the face and back up again, bash the lip, careen downward once again while executing a 180-degree turn, drive the stern of the boat deep into the trough at the bottom of the wave, loop backward, snap 120 degrees to become parallel with the wave, fling his or her upper torso downwave into a barrel roll, carve a U-turn and rocket back up the wave, dance on top of the lip until the cornice collapses, drop back down the wave once more to regain speed, and then shoot out laterally just before the wave plays out. When you start making moves like this, it's time to show up at the kayak surf contests and compete with the big dogs.

Endless Summer

When the wind kicks up, even relatively protected bodies of water like the Great Lakes or the Gulf of Mexico are sometimes transformed into exciting surf playgrounds. Tidal rips, maelstroms, and standing waves generated by fast-flowing rivers can also be wild places to test your paddling spirit. Nothing will hone your sea kayaking skills faster than surfing in breaking water. Proficiency in the surf zone could become a lifesaver on an exposed-coast expedition or when you venture into a rock garden or a sea cave. If you love excitement, get out there and dance with the waves every chance you get. A skilled, courageous kayak surfer can go almost anywhere waves are breaking.

A good way to learn surf kayaking is to take a class from a reputable club or private instructor. Before surfing, be sure to view the instructional video, *Surf Kayaking Fundamentals.* Also, pore over the book *Nigel Foster's Surf Kayaking* to gather useful information about paddling in the surf. (See chapter 11, "Resources.")

Exposed Coast and Open Ocean

> **Since time began, the old ones have spoken of a distant coast where game and sunlight were in such abundance, that those who discovered this place never returned.**
> —Old Aleutian legend

Inuit and Aleut sea kayakers braved formidable northern seas in pursuit of wild game. G. H. von Langsdorff, visiting the Alaskan coast in 1814, observed, "These baidarkas are the best means yet discovered by mankind to go from place to place."

Modern kayakers have kept the art and adventure of sea paddling alive, sometimes venturing great distances from shore. Franz Romer and Hannes Lindemann each crossed

Eric Soares explores the rocky coast of southern Oregon during an expedition.

the Atlantic. It took Ed Gillet 63 days to paddle solo all the way from California to Hawaii in his specially equipped tandem sea kayak. Derek Hutchinson and friends paddled twice across the North Sea in narrow British kayaks, the "butterflies of the sea." The crossing was over 100 miles. Hutchinson said, "The first time we suffered vomiting, dehydration, hallucinations, nausea and hypothermia. In fact, we almost croaked." They crossed again the following year in 31 hours and set a Guinness world record.

Wayne Haack circled the Queen Charlotte Islands off the coast of British Columbia, Greg Blanchette explored the Hawaiian archipelago, and Valerie Fons and Verlen Krueger paddled the lengthy coast of the Baja peninsula. Paul Caffyn accomplished a whole series of rigorous sea journeys in his kayak, paddling around New Zealand, Tasmania, Japan, and Great Britain, exploring along the seacoast of Alaska, and then circumnavigating the entire Australian continent—a stupendous feat.

A multiday sea kayaking journey, whether along a wilderness coast or across an expanse of open water, is truly a great adventure. Many sea kayakers, once they have gained experience with surf, wind, and weather, begin dreaming of venturing farther and farther out to sea. *Sea Kayaker* magazine and a few good books (e.g., John Dowd's classic manual, *Sea Kayaking*), offer a cornucopia of useful information on various aspects of exposed-coast and open-sea paddling (see chapter 11, "Resources"). Planning an expedition, what to take and how to pack it in your boat, camping while sea kayaking, and even how to prepare mentally and psychologically for a long sea journey are addressed in these publications. Our focus here is on the challenges and skills of paddling in open seas and along exposed coasts with a laden boat.

Storm Sea Kayaking

Paddling in good weather, across an expanse of gently rolling seas beneath an open sky, can seem quite carefree. No half-submerged rocks or breaking waves out here, like near the shore. But when the weather turns wild, that's another story.

As boys growing up in the mountains far from the sea, we read Edgar Allen Poe's "A Descent into the Maelstrom." The poet's vivid description of a hapless mariner swept into a swirling whirlpool awakened in our young minds a lasting fascination with the wild side of the sea. Decades later, Michael and a film crew would have the opportunity to paddle in the midst of raging Saltstraumen maelstrom in northern Norway and record the experience with waterproof movie cameras.

Intrepid kayakers have braved the open sea for days at a time, sometimes facing conditions as terrifying as any maelstrom. Franz Romer succeeded in paddling across the Atlantic in 1928, the first person known to complete such a feat. He made it all the way from Portugal to Puerto Rico in eight weeks, only to disappear in a Caribbean hurricane shortly thereafter.

Hannes Lindemann crossed the Atlantic twice, first in a dugout canoe in 1955 and later in a folding boat like Romer's in 1956. In Will Nordby's *Seekers of the Horizon*, an anthology of sea kayaking sagas, Lindemann recalls days of struggling through heavy seas during his second voyage (see chapter 11, "Resources"). He capsized twice but refused to give up. "Once I narrowly missed disaster," he later wrote. "An enormous breaker, coming from the rear, left me gasping for air as it poured water into the

boat. We were taken thirty to forty-five feet high into the air and then flung down with a hard bump." Lindemann says he survived those 72 days at sea by practicing self-hypnosis. He also possessed exceptional kayaking skills and was properly outfitted.

Preparation for Stormy Weather Paddling

Any exposed-coast kayaker should be prepared to get caught at sea in wild weather. You may wonder, what is it like, paddling a tiny boat in a big storm? Spend enough time at sea, and there's a good chance you may find out.

As for other requirements of extreme-condition sea kayaking, it's preferable to be a strong paddler and possess endurance to paddle mile after mile alone in frothing seas. A stable, somewhat willful mind is essential to prevent yourself from going crazy in the constant stimuli. Reliable paddling skills are also important, especially surf-zone experience. Still, the only sure way to develop reliable storm sea kayaking ability is to get out when things are wild and go for it.

Sometimes, when conditions are too rough for surfing or rock garden play, we elect to go storm sea kayaking. Although this is usually initiated as a team effort, be aware that under conditions this chaotic, chances are good that you will end up alone for periods of time. That's why it's crucial that *everyone* in a group preparing to venture out into a storm sea be a skilled kayaker.

What is meant by "storm conditions," anyway? Huge, confused seas and strong, gusting winds, to start with. Watch for red flags erected above harbor patrol and Coast Guard offices. A single red pennant indicates a small craft warning, and two flags flying warn of gale conditions. Rain is bearable (you will be totally drenched, regardless), but never go out if you see lightning.

Under such conditions, proper preparation becomes crucial to safety. Put on enough neoprene and polypro to insulate you from the cold. Don't forget your head, hands, and feet, especially when heading out to paddle in a more extreme climate. Michael traveled to the southern tip of Chile to explore the glacier-filled fjords of Tierra del

Alan Hillesheim kayaks in a storm at Point Lobos.

Jim Kakuk

Paddling into the Wind

It's generally easier to maintain control when paddling straight into a strong wind than when going with it. Facing the full power of a raging tempest, upper body bent forward, head down, paddle slashing into the chaos and frenzy all around, headwinds and swells racing by, is truly an exhilarating feeling. Even if waves are breaking over your bow and you are making negligible headway, you are likely to feel in control. There's little opportunity to pause and rest while paddling upwind, however. Even though it may feel like you are flying, chances are you've made little progress, and the moment you stop paddling you will find yourself being blown backward. If your landing objective is still upwind, that can be a serious problem. You may have no choice but to keep paddling, hard and steady, until you reach it. If your put-in/take-out site is downwind, stop paddling against the wind before you get tired, so you'll have energy left to run with the wind.

Running with the Wind

Running with the weather can be more tricky than paddling against it. Inexperienced kayakers capsize more often when wind and waves are at their backs. The first warning of a wind-driven wave rolling up behind is often when the stern of your boat gets lifted suddenly skyward. Here is where those hours you spent in the surf zone pay off. If your boat is too far forward on the wave, your bow may be driven down into the trough ahead. Respond by throwing your upper torso back, on to the rear deck. Unless the wave is too big, this should push your stern back down and put the brakes on.

Fuego by kayak. He brought along neoprene booties and sailing gloves that worked fine in California, but he found them inadequate for paddling comfort in a frigid climate. In extreme or remote conditions, a PFD equipped with a strobe light, EPIRB (emergency position-indicating radio beacon), and aerial flares and with an outside pocket where a high-calorie energy bar or drink can be stashed is appropriate.

Be sure to eat a high-calorie meal and drink plenty of water before you launch in stormy conditions, and make sure to stow a bottle of additional drinking water within easy reach. When the wind is strong, ballast in the bottom center and just inside the bow may improve a kayak's stability. Before launching, ensure that your boat's float bags are fully inflated and all deck hatches are secured. Some expedition paddlers have experimented with setting out a drogue or sea chute to slow their drift in a big wind, but we don't practice this because of the risk of entanglement when setting 100 feet of line during a howling storm.

Launch from a protected beach or harbor when paddling on a really rough day. Then, linger for a while in the protected area if possible, to get warmed up and tuned in and to ensure you can paddle against the wind before heading out to more exposed water. If your plan is to return to where you launched at the end of the paddle, *always* paddle against the wind on the way out and with the wind on the way back. *Never* make the grievous error of going miles downwind while fresh and then battling back against the wind when exhausted.

If you sense a set of surfable swells rolling up behind you and want to take advantage of their energy to accelerate your forward motion, paddle hard and lean forward each time you feel your stern being lifted by a wave. Then surf for as long as you can, by leaning forward or back and executing forward or reverse paddle strokes as needed, to keep your planing boat in just the right place on the front of the wave. Sometimes you can go for hundreds of meters in this way with hardly any effort, when the wind and swells are solidly behind you, even when paddling a laden boat.

Some kayakers with sailing experience stow a kite, umbrella, or small sailing rig (perhaps even a genoa jib or spinnaker) in their cockpit to deploy when paddling long distances in wind that is consistent but not too strong. For the uninitiated, kiting or sailing can be more trouble than it's worth, but it can be a godsend when traveling great distances downwind. In big winds, stow the sailing rig, straighten your posture, and use your back as a sail. It works.

Whether you plane or sail downwind, recall the sailor's sendoff: "May you have fair winds and following seas." Running with the wind is the ideal for sailboats and should be for kayaks also. The trick is to get out there and practice.

Reaching

Even accomplished kayakers sometimes flounder in a strong side wind. Lined up parallel to the swells and perpendicular to the wind, you'll find staying upright a major chore. As the wind velocity approaches 30 knots, the smallest paddling error can capsize a kayak. But sometimes there's no other choice, no other way home except to paddle with a strong, buffeting wind from the side.

When *reaching* (paddling with the wind coming across your beam), lean your upper body into the wind but stay alert and ready to compensate for fast-changing conditions. Even when the wind velocity is consistent, sudden changes in wind speed will occur

The Storm Sea King

We first met on a dark and stormy winter day in 1983. I was winding my way up the Mendocino coast in northern California, searching for a place to surf with my river kayak. Driving through the little town of Elk, I spotted a big washdeck torpedo of a kayak lying out in front of a dilapidated warehouse. I stepped from my car, and a towering giant of a man emerged from the rustic structure to greet me. He introduced himself as Steve Sinclair, boat seller, kayaking guide and instructor, and head of a tribe of local storm surf paddlers, aptly named Force Ten.

Steve's infectious enthusiasm soon won me over. He described what it was like to kayak miles offshore in a winter gale. "It's like helicopter blades out there, man." He expounded his kayak philosophy, accompanied by extravagant gestures:

1. The ocean is big and wild, and where it's at.

2. Ya gotta be a waterman, first and foremost.

3. Washdeck kayaks are the only way to go.

4. Helmets and full wetsuits are a must.

5. Kayak often and live a life of freedom.

"Eirikur!" he bellowed, and the ancient wooden walls of the warehouse reverberated. Just being in the presence of this great Viking spirit struck a chord deep within me, and we soon became fast friends. Sinclair inspired me to cut loose and expand my horizons in the ocean.

I bought one of their hand-built Odyssea Surf Skis and began to emulate the Force Ten style of paddling. My lifelong friend Jim Kakuk and I formed our own kayaking team and called it the Tsunami Rangers. The Force Ten group and the Rangers competed in grueling, 7-mile coastal races. Steve was the fastest, most powerful, most skilled, most courageous paddler of us all. Time after time, we watched, astounded, as the founder of storm sea kayaking charged straight toward a monstrous, breaking comber—and the waves parted for him. Steve loved nothing better than paddling out in the open sea with subhurricane winds and 20-foot swells roaring around him. He overtook sailboats struggling in the wind and saved swimmers ensnared by dangerous surf. He showed other sea kayakers that paddling in stormy conditions on purpose was possible and very fun.

(continued on page 68)

Will Nordby

Steve Sinclair, founder of Force Ten, a pioneer storm sea kayaker.

(continued from page 67)

Will Nordby

Steve Sinclair heads out into the storm.

Steve passed away in 1996 but left a legacy of speaking the truth about the risks of sea kayaking and extending the boundaries of kayaking in extreme seas. I miss this pioneer, this instigator, this man who loved the sea and was loved by the sea. As I paddle up the mighty waves and through the spindrift, I follow the spirit of a consummate waterman—Steve Sinclair, the Storm Sea King.

—Eric

when you go from deep troughs to the tops of waves. Execute quick slap braces and sculling strokes to stay upright and on course. If it is necessary to turn your boat around and reach the other way, head downwind initially, so you can gather speed to make the turn. In the event of capsize, roll back up on the windward side, so the wind will assist rather than hinder your effort.

Expedition Kayaking

There are two basic kinds of sea kayaking expeditions—open-sea crossings and paddling exposed coasts. Many extreme-condition coastal paddlers we know believe that slogging along day after day on the open sea is so boring, it is hardly worth

doing. However, the open sea is not always a recipe for ennui.

Once, on a navy warship, Eric endured two days of thrashing through a super typhoon in the Philippine Straits. The 300-foot ship rolled, pitched, yawed, lurched, creaked, shivered, and groaned in the 130-knot winds and 70-foot waves until it seemed it would tear apart. Eric reckoned these conditions were far too severe for anyone in a tiny craft to survive.

Open-Sea Crossings
The Tsunami Rangers hope to paddle across the Bering Strait from North America to Asia some day in support of the proposed Beringian Heritage International Park. Unlike soloists Romer, Lindemann, and Ed Gillet, the Rangers would make the crossing a team effort. Although the water gap between Alaska and Russia is only 90 miles wide, it poses a formidable threat to small boat navigation. The strait is an area of relatively shallow water, where tremendous pressures generated by the interaction between the Arctic Ocean and the Bering Sea cause currents, waves, and brash ice to surge back and forth chaotically. Kayaking across such a tumultuous expanse of open water demands careful planning, acquisition of navigational skills, being in top paddling condition, and good luck.

Exploring the Exposed Coast
Traveling along an exposed coast is another exciting type of extreme sea kayaking expedition. Some coastal kayakers paddle from point to point and cover great distances, sometimes as much as 30 miles a day or more. Thomas Mann describes the phenomenon: "The coastwise voyager finds no

The Channel Islands Debacle

Ed Gillet asked me in 1986 if I wanted to paddle from California to Hawaii with him. "It'll just be a sailing expedition," Ed said. "Forty days, max." I declined on the grounds that it seemed like a lot of work and not particularly exciting. As it turned out, the trade winds never materialized, forcing Ed to paddle alone all the way to Hawaii in 1987. It took him 63 days.

I might have accepted Ed's offer, except for an ill-fated paddle from the southern California coast to the Channel Islands. Ever since then, I have avoided open sea crossings. Here's the story.

In May of 1986, Rangers Alan Hillesheim, Jim Kakuk, and I decided to paddle out and explore the Channel Islands. We realized we needed to gain open-sea experience because we also dreamed of paddling to Hawaii with an armada of kayaks. We asked permission to paddle to Santa Cruz Island and camp, but park officials turned us down. So, we opted for a commando-style crossing instead, to another island in the same group—Santa Rosa Island, just 32 statute miles from the California mainland. Our plan was to paddle there under cover of darkness, camouflage our camp, and surreptitiously explore the island's rock gardens and sea caves.

We should have realized that our plan was hexed when the ranger at Gaviota wouldn't let us camp or even park at the mainland campground because we lacked a reservation. But we found a place to leave our vehicle (a mile from the campground) and readied our boats. The ranger asked where we were headed. "Santa Barbara," I fibbed. We launched late in the afternoon and dutifully headed east toward Santa Barbara. We landed again as soon as we were out of sight and hid our boats until dark; then we set off again on our true journey.

We decided to paddle at night to maximize our chances of making the crossing undetected. Aside from a compass, we carried no navigation equipment. After napping, we launched under a new moon. Puffing my way into what looked like some easy 2-foot surf, I got surprised by a dumper wave that fire-hosed me against my back deck. After we all had made it through the surf, we rafted up. Everyone was soaked, although Alan still appeared sleepy.

We formed into an inverted-V tight formation to begin the 32-mile crossing to Santa Rosa Island. We were heading into a busy shipping channel, in the dark, and now it was getting foggy. Ah, well. With a light breeze at our backs, we continued on our southerly course in good spirits. All went fine for a few hours. Visions of Hawaii danced through our heads. Sleepyhead Alan kept drifting out of formation, so we put him up front.

At dawn, we rafted up to wolf down peanut butter sandwiches and washed them down with a liter of cranberry juice spiked with weightlifter's carbohydrate powder. It was barely edible, but we were hungry. Alan refused to drink the purple stuff. His loss, I thought.

We continued on through the dense early morning fog and passed alertly through the shipping channel, our senses tuned to the ships we heard in front and behind us. It was scary. After negotiating the channel and traveling what we figured was about 17 miles, we rafted up for a briefing.

I was feeling sicker than a dog. Swallowing bile, Jim admitted he, too, was just a wee bit under the weather. Alan felt great! We debated the merits of continuing versus turning back. Jim cautioned us to return to Gaviota while we still had strength. He reasoned that he and I might be suffering from food poisoning (Tsunami Rangers couldn't be seasick; no way), and things could get even worse for us if we stayed out here in these rolling seas. Besides, at best we would be stuck on a remote island with no medical facilities. That is, if we were fortunate enough to find Santa Rosa Island in this chicken gravy fog.

Alan was the lone voice arguing to continue. He reasoned that paddling on toward our invisible objective in following seas would be quicker and easier than heading back across that dreaded shipping channel in the fog. He expounded that this was a rehearsal for an even grander adventure at sea, and overcoming adversity was an admirable virtue and a major feature of the Tsunami creed. Yeah, Alan felt disgustingly great.

I sincerely believed that Alan should be promoted to lieutenant commander for his cogent argument, courage, leadership, and initiative. Nevertheless, I sided with Jim and wheezed, "Let's get out of here."

We turned back into the wind and the waves. More hours passed, and we trudged along through the sea dunes and prayed for the fog to lift so we could catch a glimpse of our salvation, the mainland. We plowed right across the shipping channel, ignoring the sounds of the freighters. Then the fog cleared, and we saw Point Conception looming ahead. This finger of land a scant 12 miles ahead was a joyous sight.

(continued on page 70)

(continued from page 69)

We paused to rest. While one of us kept the kayaks rafted up together, the others slipped off our open cockpit boats and swam around to stretch our aching muscles. Then we lumbered onward, Jim leading stoically, me wallowing along behind him, and Alan sweeping. During those final hours, I sang "Three Waves to Go," a hypnotic reggae verse based on a Bob Marley medley.

The song comforted me. I thought about our planned journey to Hawaii and realized that then I would be singing "Three Million Waves to Go." I reassured myself that I would never, ever paddle to Hawaii. After 34 miles and 9 hours of paddling, we arrived at Hollister Ranch, a beautiful stretch of beach adorned with expensive vacation homes. We collapsed on the sand for a nap but were soon awakened by a security guard with a face as lovable as a French pug, ordering us to leave. Not feeling like arguing about mean high tide and other esoteric principles, we launched and limped back to Gaviota Beach, where a ranger waited with folded arms. Since the Channel Islands debacle, the Tsunami Rangers choose their adventures more wisely and prefer to remain within sight of the mainland shore.

—Eric

end to his journey, for behind each headland of clayey dune he conquers, fresh headlands and new distances lure him on."

It is quite an achievement to paddle vast distances from headland to headland, except you miss out on the coast. It's the same as driving your car across America in two days. You accomplish a lot but don't see much of the countryside while traveling 75 mph on the freeways. Plus you are exhausted when you reach your destination. Is this fun?

Unlike the person drawn to the next headland, we embrace a more microcosmic style of coastal exploration. Each year the Tsunami Rangers organize a week-long paddling retreat and explore a stretch of remote, scenic coastline, up close and personal. Typically, we may travel only 30 linear miles along a coast during one of these expeditions. But during that time, we

A team of Tsunami Rangers on an expedition in southern Oregon.

investigate sea caves and blow holes, travel to interesting rock formations to discover exciting play spots, paddle through an inviting sea arch, and ride waves breaking onto a hidden microbeach that may never have been surfed before. We band together to battle around a dangerous headland but then disburse again to explore a protected stretch of shoreline in search of a good campsite, a tide pool area rich in abalone, or an exposed reef covered with succulent mussels for dinner.

Launching and Landing on the Exposed Coast

When launching or landing in exposed conditions, especially with laden boats, it's always wise to operate as a team. Practice the principles of surf-zone etiquette discussed in the previous chapter.

Look around for sea stacks, reefs, or other barriers

> Exploring the outer Vesterålen archipelago in arctic Norway.

that might shelter your route from the full impact of the breaking surf. A strong rip current could make approaching a beach difficult but would probably make launching through a surf zone eas-

ier. Look for a route where the chance of being driven onto rocks by breaking waves is minimized. One of the strongest and best equipped paddlers in a team should lead the way in and out through a rock garden or surf zone and then turn to signal to the others when it's safe to proceed. The most heavily laden boats and the least experienced paddlers should go next, with another strong kayaker going in or out last.

Choosing a Campsite on the Exposed Coast

On an exposed coast, it's crucial to find a campsite that is protected from wind, breaking waves, and high tides. Along a mountainous shoreline, it's also important to watch out for unstable cliffs that may loom above. Camping along one of our favorite stretches of the spectacular coast in southern Oregon, we have narrowly escaped disaster twice when big rocks tumbled down onto the beach during rain storms. Moments after John Lull left his tent to join the others around the morning fire, a football-shaped rock crashed through the top of his tent and destroyed his *saxophone* on one of these trips.

Avoid pocket beaches bordered by steep cliffs, where big surf and a rising tide could entrap you and wash out your camp. Use topographic maps to locate good camping spots because they show detailed land features such as gradient. The ideal campsite is situated well above the high-tide line, is hidden from civilization, has abundant water and wood, and has an escape route.

Once a good campsite is established, supplies can be off-loaded and left behind while the team explores an area on a series of day-paddles in empty boats. A nearby rock garden, the subject of the next chapter, can be more easily and safely explored this way. But before we look more closely at rock gardens, let's first journey north of the Arctic Circle and kayak a wild, exposed coast in the wake of the Vikings.

Paddling the Rugged
Coast of Northern Norway

We stared out at the primal fury of Saltstraumen maelstrom from the banks of Skjerstadfjorden in northern Norway. With each tidal change, 400 million cubic meters of seawater would turn and sweep through a narrow channel. Now in the boiling whitewater a few yards away, colossal whirlpools and standing waves formed and then disappeared just as suddenly.

I asked Frank Jacobsen, a local paddler whose skills had been honed in arctic storms and Class 5 rapids on Scandinavian rivers, if anyone had ever run the maelstrom in a kayak. "No, I'm afraid that would be suicidal," he answered solemnly. Still, the lure of paddling unchallenged Saltstraumen lingers, and I dream of attempting it someday.

The south of Norway is blessed with warm summers, 800-year-old stave churches, and the burial sites of Viking kings and their legendary long boats. Yet it was to the far north that I felt drawn, up beyond the Arctic Circle to the Land of the Midnight Sun. From this rugged coast, my grandmother had come to America a century ago. Over the years, I'd heard tales of the wild beauty of the Lofoten and Vesterålen archipelago, where some of the world's oldest mountains thrust far out into the tempestuous Norwegian Sea. Here, whales and orcas patrolled deep fjords in pursuit of herring and salmon, and countless puffins, auks, and other seabirds swarmed from high cliffs and turned the sky black. Warmed by the Gulf Stream yet repeatedly swept by fierce arctic storms, these mountainous emerald islands formed a weather fence between the northern ice cap and continental Europe, a meteorological battlefield where great tropical and polar forces battled with explosive force.

Midsummer was fast approaching when a Scandinavian Airlines jet bore me north along the ragged Norwegian coastline to the town of Bodø, about 80 kilometers above the Arctic Circle. There I met Frank and Heidi, another member of the Bodø Kajakk Klubb. Over dinner that night at a little restaurant steeped in old-world charm, they invited me to join them in exploring the islands scattered farther north along the roadless coast. The kayak club provided me with a sleek Finnish-made craft, appropriately called a Viking. The next morning Heidi and I went to buy provisions, and soon we were racing north through the islands on a high-speed passenger boat. Landing on Engeløy (øy at the end of a name designates a place as an island), or Angel Island, we were met by her friend Inge, who would join us in the paddle north.

The sun had fallen low in the sky by the time we had finished stuffing our kayaks with camping gear and a week's worth of food. When I grew anxious about reaching our first campsite before dark, Heidi and Inge both chuckled. "The sun won't set for two more months," Inge gently reminded me.

Our plan was to paddle north to the island of Lundøy, which Heidi recalled had a cove where we could establish a base camp for subsequent explorations. But a stiff headwind rose to challenge us as soon as we reached open water, and choppy seas began breaking over the plunging bows of our kayaks. I had to stroke mightily to keep up with the Norwegians. Their passion for racing at top speed through rough waters probably evolved from those days when their Viking ancestors delighted in chasing down hapless prey in the sea, I mused. To complicate matters further, I discovered the unfamiliar left-hand control paddle (right-hand control paddles apparently didn't exist in Norway) a challenge to use. Fortunately, the boat I paddled proved swift and stable, and later that evening we drew near the green mountains of Lundøy.

Our camp was a grassy meadow at the back of the well-protected cove, through which a stream wound to the sea. A seagull sat serenely on her nest, surrounded by wildflowers, a few yards from my tent. The mountains rose up steeply at the edge of the meadow. Other friends of Heidi and Inge's arrived from the south, until nine kayaks lay nestled in the tall grass above the high-tide line at the edge of camp.

In the endless arctic summer days ahead, my new friends led me on a series of extraordinary adventures among the surrounding islands. One morning we paddled back to the sparsely settled western side of Engeløy to search for some old Viking grave sites that Inge had heard about. After hiking a way along the shore, we spotted several ancient circles of stone in a field. "Those are the women's graves," Inge gestured, "and the men's are over there." A monolith of weathered granite marked the burial site of an important chieftain. Nearby we discovered the crumbling remains of some old stone boathouses. Even in eternal rest, the Vikings and their ships were never far apart.

One morning I hiked away from camp alone, intent on exploring the lush green mountains that rose above us. A few steps from the sun-splashed meadow I found myself immersed in a low-canopied forest, thickly carpeted with moss and ferns. The feeling here was mysterious, and I almost expected to stumble across Odin's half-buried sword or glimpse a troll peering out at me from some dark recess of the understory.

Ravenous from a long day of climbing, I descended back to camp that evening to find Inge crouched over an open fire. He was tending a pot of stew, from which rose a tantalizing, yet unfamiliar, aroma. "Whale," he announced, conscious of the reaction of many Americans to the hunting of this traditional Norwegian food. He had explained to me previously that only a small quota of the now abundant minke whales are taken for domestic consumption. I must admit that in the context of this wilderness coast up beyond the Arctic Circle and in the company of these strong, high-spirited descendants of the Vikings, whose rugged, outdoor lifestyle I'd come to admire, issues of political correctness seemed remote and somehow irrelevant.

A few days later we returned to Bodø. Now I made my way even further north, into the fabled Lofoten and Vesterålen Islands that I had dreamed of visiting for so many years. I joined a group, led by American outfitter Tim Conlan and his Swedish wife, Lena, to attempt reaching the outer fringes of the rugged archipelago in kayaks. Beneath ominous skies, we launched from the quaint little port town of Stokmarknes, our boats heavily laden for an extended wilderness exploration. In the days that followed, when conditions allowed, we would dash from island to island across stretches of open water and then run for protection in one of the numerous deep fjords whenever playful Thor decided to unleash another fusillade of lashing rain and thunder. Tim consulted his topographic maps and charts frequently, searching for the safest route through the labyrinth. One day, to avoid the exposed, north-facing coast of a big island called Langøy, we paddled into the shadow of appropriately named Vindhammaren (Wind Hammer) and made camp by a roaring mountain stream at the upper end of a fjord. The next morning we portaged our kayaks across a narrow pass to the head of another fjord that led to the opposite side of the island.

In this way, we progressed through the wild Vesterålen Islands and developed a wonderful feeling of connectedness with the ancient Vikings in whose wake we followed. The islands of northern Norway are arguably the most beautiful place I've ever drawn a kayak paddle through the sea.

—Michael

If You Want to Go

Tim and Lena Conlan are the only outfitters I know who offer guided sea kayaking trips into the wilderness areas of northern Norway and Sweden. Some of these trips are exploratory and quite challenging. Both Tim and Lena are seasoned wilderness guides, and Lena was born in Sweden. For information on their company, Crossing Latitudes, see chapter 11, "Resources."

In addition, the Norwegian Tourist Board (NORTRA) is a good resource for maps and information about adventure travel options in Norway. Nordland Reiseliv is the official tourist agency of Nordland, the part of northern Norway encompassing the Lofoten and Vesterålen archipelagos. For further information, see chapter 11, "Resources."

—Michael

7 Ocean Rock Gardens

> " Grok the rock. "
>
> —Diego Cienfuegos, ocean philosopher

Have you ever gazed into a painting of powerful waves sweeping across a jagged coastline and imagined yourself paddling there? Perhaps you think it is too dangerous to realistically picture yourself cavorting in flying surf, dodging rocks and waves, caught up in the chaotic froth of one of the earth's great power spots—the meeting of land and sea. Being prudent, you may never have dreamed of venturing into such dangerous circumstances. But given the proper training, and in the company of experienced companions, you could paddle it. If people can kayak rock-strewn rivers, why not rock-strewn seascapes?

The dangers of paddling in rock gardens are real. These are places where powerful natural forces are concentrated and expend tremendous energy. Here you could crash into a rock and break your boat. But as you gain experience and skill, the hazards lessen and the thrills and enjoyment grow greater. In the pages ahead, we delve into how to paddle among sea stacks, rocky headlands, and open sea reefs, some of the most spectacular and beautiful features of a wilderness coastline.

A Closer Look at that Seascape Painting

As discussed in chapter 4, scouting the terrain you intend to paddle is helpful, especially when preparing to explore ocean rock gardens that lie exposed to big waves. All the perils of the surf zone are present, on a collision course with hard, uncompromising rock in its many forms. Before setting off down an unknown coast, it's useful to study large-scale topographic maps and navigational charts of the area. Take note of beaches, protected landing sites, and any special hazards, such as where asterisks are printed on marine charts to indicate rocks and sea stacks. Before launching, take your binoculars and hike up to a high vantage point; take a good look around. With amplified vision, you can locate play spots and detect danger zones without placing yourself in harm's way. From your elevated position, you can envision yourself making your moves in the varying conditions seen through the binoculars.

Once on the water, remain vigilant for breaking waves or even subtle changes in the surface of the sea that may reveal dangers looming ahead. Don't move into a rock garden until you see a safe route through. Observe what happens when breakers thunder onshore. Is there enough calm time to paddle through an area between waves or sets of waves? Are there protected zones to duck into if a big set catches you inside? Could a capsized or disabled paddler get out of there? On the plus side, are there exciting play spots or beautiful vistas that make it worthwhile to venture in there in the first place?

Whitewater river kayakers who first come to paddle in ocean rock gardens soon learn that different forces are at work here. While waves in a river rapids remain stationary, in the sea they travel, sometimes for great distances, before breaking against a shoreline or offshore reef. Likewise, hydraulics (holes) in river rapids remain pretty much in the same place and unchanged, at least until the flow level of the river changes. River features are linear and stable.

However, in the ocean, everything is jazzy. A big suckhole may develop suddenly in an ocean rock garden when a wave withdraws, and then it might vanish moments later beneath a flood of oncoming water as the next wave crashes in. In the sea, waves generally arrive in sets, and waves of much different sizes can come within the same set. You never know what you are going to get.

Robert Heinlein's term to *grok*, meaning to gain total understanding of a situation in an instant, is appropriate here. Capable ocean rock garden kayakers soon learn to grok the waves and the rocks. They employ TNT (tuning 'n' timing) to increase their awareness and safety. Wherever big surf breaks over rocks, windows of opportunity can be brief, and these skills become immensely valuable. Learning to tune in and to grok will enable you to recognize the right moment to make your move.

Four Rock Garden Zones

As you mosey down the corridors of sea stacks, washover rocks, suckholes, and barely submerged reefs, it is crucial to recognize danger zones and transition routes that will enable you to avoid traps, reach areas of safety, and find fun, safe places to play. Let's look at these four types of zones.

A *safe zone* is a place in a rock garden that affords protection from big waves, prevailing winds, and strong currents. Safe zones are typically located on the landward side of big rocks or sea stacks, and the best ones may feature an impression or miniature cove big enough for you and your companions to slip into.

A *transition zone* is a route you take to move safely from one area to another area. For example, if you are outside a reef and exposed to powerful, breaking surf, you may need to paddle a convoluted route to reach a protected zone at the other side of a rock garden. This might entail waiting for a break in a succession of big waves, dashing across a dangerous area, and then cutting behind a rock for protection before another breaking wave arrives. The trick is to be aware that you are transiting, and this takes TNT.

Jim Kakuk and Eric Soares transit through breaking surf to reach a safe zone behind a rock.

I Just Dropped Into Position

Jim Kakuk and I once paddled near the base of a high cliff on the northern California coast. Each time a set of waves rolled in, we swung around to face them and remained parallel to each other. When a particularly big wave arrived, we powered forward to punch through, felt the rush of briefly getting airborne, quickly followed by a Bagwan whump as the wave exploded on the wall behind us and sent spray high in the air. During a pause between sets, Jim skittered in front of me to cross to the protective lee of a nearby rock. He tuned, timed, and transited, but he misjudged the arrival and size of the next wave. The wave had split in two as it refracted around a rock in front of us; then it reformed, reared up, and broke on Jim, sending him flying sideways, directly toward me. I couldn't back up since the cliff was directly behind me.

I deftly shot forward a bit so Jim's hull would crash on my foredeck, near the bow. The collision arrested Jim's sideways progress and saved my thorax, but the impact forced the nose of my boat down into a forward endo and flip over. Jim scurried out of harm's way, but I was dragged upside down through a sluice and into a protected tidal pool. My paddle was jerked from my grasp, so I released my seat belt and popped to the surface. I flipped my boat back up, remounted, and used my hands to scramble through the spent surf to deep water before the next wave came in. I was too wiped out and shook up to think about retrieving my paddle. When things settled down a bit, Jim dashed back in and scooped it up.

After the incident, we figured out that Jim had been surprised by the wave, which appeared rather small and weak but suddenly doubled in size and strength when a side wave joined it in a compressed area. Once the wave had curled up and started to break over us, our immediate response was to attempt to minimize the collision damage, which we did. There was no way I was going to let Jim hit me full force and then have both of us slam backward into the cliff.

Though our quick responses saved us, in retrospect we realized there were several things we could have done better. Had we scouted the area more thoroughly before we paddled in there, we might have perceived that spot more as a danger zone than a play spot. If Jim's TNT would have been better, he would have attempted his transit at a more propitious moment. If we had fanned out at the outset, the collision may not have happened at all. We resolved in the future to always grok what position our position was in!

—Eric

A *danger zone* is a place where you could get hurt or could risk damaging or losing your boat. In danger zones, waves break hard onto jagged rocks, and escape or rescue is difficult. To the untrained, a danger zone may initially look like a play spot or safe place. This is when careful scouting from a safe zone could save the day. The area may be a docile kitten one moment and change to a charging tiger the next. Remain vigilant and live a long, happy life.

A *play spot* is a zone of dramatic interaction between waves and rocks, where exciting paddling moves can be attempted with reasonable safety. Spectacular maneuvers, tricks, stunts, advanced paddling techniques, and just plain fun can all be enjoyed here. Remain aware, though, that the distinction between a play spot and a danger zone can be marginal or can disappear entirely when a big set of waves thunders in unexpectedly. Recognizing and responding to danger at play spots is a continuing challenge for extreme-condition kayakers. We consider some different types of play spots later in this chapter.

Positioning

Transiting smoothly from one zone to another demands careful *positioning*— establishing yourself in the most advantageous place with the least amount of effort. Skillful positioning, coupled with good **TNT**, will help you avoid a lot of perilous situations within rock gardens.

Imagine you are nestled in the lee of a big rock. If a side wave or powerful surge threatens to push you into danger, a series of quick ninja strokes forward, backward, and to the side can help you maintain your position and avoid wedges, sharp rocks, fellow boaters,

and anything else you don't want to run into. When a big set of waves crashes and creates a washing machine environment, relax your body, do reflexive slap braces to stay upright, and go with the energy.

When sharing a play zone with other kayakers, be careful to position yourselves so incoming waves will not throw you into one other. Generally, this requires remaining parallel to each other, rather than perpendicular, and fanning out in a row facing the waves, rather than lining up in a column. If a rock stands between you and the open sea, paddle in close to it for shelter from the initial impact when a big wave hits, but be ready to deal with the chaos when the two sections of the wave roll around both sides of the rock and converge again. Skillful positioning is essential in an exposed rock garden.

Fundamental Rock Garden Techniques

Since paddling in ocean rock gardens is a more complex and potentially more hazardous activity than surfing, more skill and experience are required. Good stamina and rough-water swimming ability are essential, as are surfing skills, a reliable Eskimo roll, and experience with big seas. Rolling and self-rescue are important because, typically, reaching shore entails a long swim through a rock and whitewater obstacle course.

Surfing skills are paramount because losing control of your boat while on a big wave in a rock garden can be very dangerous. It's okay to broach on a big wave all the way onto a sandy beach through open water, but traveling sideways through a rock-littered seascape is like a steelie caroming through a pinball machine.

Last, you must be proficient in rescue techniques and be the type who responds well in tight situations. In an ocean rock garden, there will most likely be no one but you and your paddling companions to help out in an emergency.

All these factors combined are the reason for adding 20 points to the SCRS rating if you plan on playing in a rock garden. When you enter a rock zone, the difficulty rating automatically goes up a class level, say from a Class 3 surf zone to a more risky Class 4.

A good introduction to rock garden paddling is to go out during mild conditions, with experienced paddlers who can teach you the ropes, and experience gradual increments of risk. First try kayaking to the lee side of big sea stacks. Allow the mild surge to take you closer and closer to the rock while you grok the environment. When next to the stack, reach out and actually touch the rocks—first with your paddle, then with your hand. This will literally give you a better *feel* for the situation.

> **Stay parallel with each other to minimize collision damage.**

If the onshore surf is mellow enough, you might try approaching areas where cliffs rise vertically from the open sea. Ease yourself gradually closer until you can sense the energy of the waves reflecting back off the cliff faces. Once comfortable with this, move even closer, perhaps within a boat length or so of the cliffs. Keep a pillow of water between you and the rock. The pillow will cushion impact should you be pushed into the rock. Remain constantly alert for approaching waves. Should a wave appear that looks like it might break, spin your boat around and paddle hard, straight through it and out to safety.

After you have gained more confidence and experience with rock gardens, you may feel ready to paddle out and approach a *boomer*, an offshore rock with waves breaking over it. Be careful to stay in deep water and facing toward the rock on its lee side, parallel to your paddle mates.

> "In wild water, ever-changing conditions establish the rules. Getting out with only light battle scars is winning."
> —Captain Jim Kakuk

Observe how the waves hit the rock, break over it, and withdraw. The protected side of a boomer can sometimes make an ideal entry-level rock garden play spot. Waves hit the boomer and produce spray, which rains down upon you and feels good. Once acclimated, you might be ready for more challenging situations.

Then on a calm day with small surf (3 feet or less), paddle with experienced companions around to the seaward side of a rock and practice backing up, with waves rolling under you and breaking on the rock behind you. Don't hesitate to pull away if you feel the waves are too strong and might push you back into the rock. But when done right, this challenging maneuver will build your confidence, teach you timing, and help you begin to develop advanced rock garden paddling techniques.

As you begin to grow comfortable with small waves breaking among and over rocks, you can gradually move on to bigger waves, more technical rock gardens, and, ultimately, sea caves. But first, let's explore a few more essential techniques for paddling in rock gardens.

Seal Launches

Seal launches and landings, as practiced for centuries by Inuit paddlers in frigid arctic seas, are discussed by Derek Hutchinson in his informative book *Sea Canoeing*. Hutchinson's illustrations, showing a paddler in a kayak being assisted down a rock and slipping gently into the water, make it look simple, which it is. Launching off rocks is sometimes the only practical way to get into the water along some rugged stretches of coast. When a team is seal launching, a skilled kayaker goes first to demonstrate the technique. Others on the rock assist paddlers as they launch. The most skilled kayaker goes last, since no one is around to assist his or her launch.

When launching off low rocks, one merely slips gently

It takes good technique to paddle in rock gardens.

Jump launching.

into the water, much like a surfer would with a board. In a laden double, the stern paddler can stand beside the boat and shove it into the water, with the bow paddler already sitting aboard. The stern paddler then jumps in, or on, at the last possible moment. It is also possible with a double kayak for an experienced paddler to swim to the back of the boat, crawl up on the back deck as the bow paddler braces or sculls to keep the craft stabilized, and mount (or wiggle inside, in the case of a closed cockpit).

If perched on a steep incline or small cliff, you may have to enter the sea from a considerable height using a technique called *jump launching*, in which you toss the boat off the perch, jump in the water after the boat, and mount it. As shown in our videos, the Tsunami Rangers have jump launched from 20 feet, but this method is not recommended as a first choice because of the danger of striking the sea bottom (for ordering information, see chapter 11, "Resources").

Before jump launching, visually inspect the depth and ensure the water is at least 10 feet deep to avoid hitting submerged rocks. To perform the maneuver, wait for a calm moment between waves, throw the boat and paddle into the water, and then leap in after them. The best time to leap is usually just as surge is starting to raise the water level. Jump feet first with your legs together, hands covering your face, chin down and your elbows in tight to your body. Enter the water leaning back slightly, so your feet strike first, followed by calves, thighs, and butt, with shoulders last. Then, retrieve your paddle, swim to your boat, mount and enter it. Never dive head first—this is

how people smash their heads onto submerged rocks, with terrible consequences.

We do not jump launch while sitting inside our boats, as some river kayakers do. This is a stupid maneuver because the air will move your boat around; you could then lose control and land awkwardly, resulting in injury. Eric once launched 15 feet off a rock in the front seat of a double sit-on-top kayak. Sure enough, the boat turned on its side in midair, Eric fell out, and the boat and the paddler in the stern seat landed on top of him, knocking the wind out of him. Lesson learned.

Seal Landings

Accomplishing a smooth seal landing in a rock garden without damage to yourself or your equipment is a satisfying experience, a rite of passage for extreme-condition sea kayakers. Deliberately allowing a wave to lift and land you on a rock requires good judgment, accurate timing, and more skill than seal launching. If a seal launch seems too dicey, you can back off and find an easier place to get in the water. But when you are cold and tired,

The 60-Foot Seal Landing

Eric Soares sets up for a seal landing in Big Sur.

During the winter of 1993, we went to Big Sur for the shooting of a National Geographic Explorer film about extreme-condition sea kayaking. Emmy award-winning adventure filmmaker Gordon Brown was directing. As the camera crew scrambled along the cliffs above us, we paddled along the rocky shoreline, looking for play spots to demonstrate our wildwater skills.

Jim Kakuk, Maura Kistler, Michael, and I sashayed over to a rock patio that looked more exquisite to us than anything in Hearst Castle down the road. Big storm waves were crashing in and exploding 60 feet up the steep cliff and then withdrawing to form a 10-foot deep suckhole at the base. The cameras were poised, and it was time to generate some dramatic rock garden action. If we could pull it off, this would be the wildest seal landing any of us had ever done, let alone seen recorded on film. But the backwash was very powerful. The landing would have to be quick and precise. Michael went for it, but after attempting to claw up the slope a few times and nearly getting creamed in the backwash, he opted out. "That's too hairy for me," he concluded.

Maura shook her head and gasped, "No way, no how."

Back-paddling out of camera range, Jim shouted, "Go for it, Soares!" Sensing those cameras rolling, I leaped into action. I rode the next wave in, didn't make it to the top of the rock, and got sucked right back. I needed a bigger wave.

Moments later, an 8-foot Godzilla roared in, and I hopped aboard. The wave hurtled me up onto the sloping deck, 60 feet above the sea. I sprang off my X-1 Rocket Boat and grabbed the bow cord. I'd done it—I'd pulled off the most spectacular seal landing ever recorded!

(continued on page 81)

it's getting dark, or you are caught inside breaking waves, a seal landing could shift from caprice to a do-or-die procedure.

To seal land, Hutchinson writes that you wait for a wave that will break "not too heavily" on the target rock. John Dowd, in his classic book on long-distance touring, *Sea Kayaking*, states that a seal landing should not be attempted if a situation looks too forbidding. Instead, he recommends paddling on to a better landing spot or even tying up to a bed of floating sea kelp and bivouacking in one's kayak.

But let's assume you've found a satisfactory spot for a seal landing (a gentle, soft incline). As the wave rolls up behind you and begins to lift your boat, paddle energetically toward the target rock. With any luck, the wave will submerge the rock by the time you arrive, and you will wash smoothly up the slope. As your forward motion slows, grab onto the rock or brace with your paddle to avoid sliding backward. As soon as the wave withdraws, quickly exit your boat and haul it to high ground before the next wave hits.

When a team of kayakers is about to attempt a seal landing together, the ablest paddler should go in first and stand ready to assist the others as they land. If you get washed back off the rock before dismounting, back-paddle energetically and withdraw before the next wave hits; then try again. With a washdeck tandem kayak, it may be easiest for the bow paddler to jump off, swim to shore, and then grab hold of the boat when the stern paddler rides up on the landing rock. In this case, the bow paddler must quickly find secure footing to avoid being swept off the rock and must take care not to get hit by the advancing boat.

When attempting to land a heavily laden

boat, or when landing in a particularly tumultuous situation, it may be safer and easier for a paddler to first swim to shore with a tow line and then pull the kayak up on a rock with an oncoming wave. When pulling a laden boat to a secure place on the rock, get assistance and keep your posture straight, knees bent, and arms close to your body so you don't strain your back.

Handling Rock Collisions

Surf etiquette and avoiding collisions with other kayakers are covered in chapter 5 and also apply to rock garden paddling. Now, let's discuss how to handle close encounters with rocks.

If you are surfing on a wave and a rock suddenly looms up in front of you, don't overreact and lose control. If you turn too abruptly, your boat will probably broach and begin bouncing along sideways, and you will have no control over the direction it goes. This exposes the bottom of your hull to collision but is still preferable to running straight into a rock at full surfing speed.

Perhaps the most dangerous thing you could do is bury your bow and pitch-pole forward, which places your head and upper torso at great risk with rocks or the shallow bottom ahead. If this does occur, perform a *Sinclair corkscrew maneuver*. For the corkscrew to be effective, act fast. In that instant when your boat begins to stand on its nose and most of the hull is free in the air, snap your hips and throw the weight of your upper torso energetically to one side. This will cause the boat to spin a half-circle in the air, which rotates your torso up and away from obstacles you are approaching, and your hull takes the beating.

Any time you capsize among rocks and waves, you must react quickly to avoid hitting your upper body on a rock. Assuming submerged rocks are nearby, it's best to roll up instantly or to paddle-vault upright in shallow water. Bailing out of your boat is preferable to remaining upside down longer than necessary in shallow water.

(continued from page 80)

Then the back surge grabbed my boat and pulled me off my feet. I felt myself being swept back toward the sea. I dove onto the top of my boat and held on while I bounced and slid down toward that awful, gaping suckhole at the base of the cliffs.

Oops! Another big wave arrived and broke over me. My boat was snatched from my grasp. I dove down and clung to a bed of mussels until the deluge swirled by. I watched helplessly as my boat went banging down through a cascade of sharp rocks.

When things settled down, I scrambled over and retrieved my battered craft. I paddled back to where Gordon was fiddling with the camera. "Dang, it sure takes a long time to load this thing," he grumbled. My 6 seconds of glory had gone unrecorded.

—Eric

If you get caught in a broach and are hurtled sideways toward the rocks, throw all the weight of your upper torso into the wave that has trapped you, and brace deeply into it with your paddle, as described in chapter 5. Relax, and just as your hull meets the rock, exhale sharply from your abdomen, making a "Ha!" sound, a *kiai*. This martial arts technique will attenuate any jarring effect on your body. With luck, your sideways-moving boat will plow up a pillow of water, which will act as a cushion between the boat and the rock. The general principle is to hit the rock with your hull, not your body.

Should you get shoved up against the rocks just as a big set is arriving, spin your boat around to face the oncoming waves. Unleash the warrior within, and power your way through them. If that fails, continue bracing and sweeping with your paddle, doing whatever it takes to stay upright and keep your upper torso away from contact with the rock. When things settle down, make a run for it.

If you cannot make it through the waves and you risk a pummeling, bail out of your boat, dive beneath each wave as it approaches, and swim along the bottom toward the open sea. Each time you surface, raise your arms to protect your face from UFOs. Repeat this process until you are past the breaking waves. You can retrieve your boat after the big set passes and conditions are safer. Remember this rule: Never get caught between a rock and a breaking wave. Protect yourself; you can always get another boat.

Should you find yourself swimming among rocks, stay attentive but relaxed. Concentrate on swimming with ease and avoiding the rocks, and quite often the waves will wash you into calmer water. If a breaking wave slams you into a rock, place your gloved hands in front of your face, palms out, and do a seal landing with your body. As you hit the rock, turn your head to the side and make the "Ha!" sound as you slap the rock with your hands close to your body, not extended. Cling to the rock as the water recedes, and get to high ground.

Haruo Hasegawa
at a blowhole.

Rocky Play Spots

Let's visit some play spots and discuss ways to have a good time out there. Wandering through rock *corridors* is rewarding as you search for perfect places to play. Here are some common play spots, presented in approximate order of difficulty. Let's start with blowholes, which are definitely dramatic but generally pretty safe to approach by kayak.

Blowholes

La Bufadora, a famous blowhole on the Baja coast near Ensenada, is an amazing spectacle when big swells are hitting. The immense power of giant waves surging through a submerged corridor is released in explosive displays rising high into the Mexican sky.

Kayakers, paddling rocky stretches of wilderness coastline, are discovering many other relatively unknown blowholes that are as spectacular as La Bufadora. Imagine hanging the bow of your kayak over Old Faithful's lip and waiting for it to erupt! But don't forget to turn your head to the side and close your eyes when a blowhole discharges like a geyser.

Minefields

Sniveler's Boneyard, as the Tsunami Rangers affectionately call a ragged, convoluted stretch of the Pacific coast near Moss Beach in northern California, is a classic rock garden *minefield*, where powerful currents and waves surge to and fro among a jumble of partially submerged offshore rocks. A minefield approximates a wildwater river in drama and complexity and provides an equally challenging and ever changing medley of extreme kayaking opportunities. To paddle through one when the sea is aroused is like running a watery gauntlet, where the rocks seem to pop up unexpectedly with each wave. A minefield is not a place for the timid or inexperienced.

Suckholes

In places where swell-energized seawater alternately breaks over rock formations and then suddenly withdraws, a *suckhole* can result. A big suckhole off Point Bonita, near the Golden Gate, is a classic example. It's easy for a kayaker to get mesmerized just by observing the surging rhythm of the sea. A favorite game that expert kayakers play in a suckhole is to follow a big wave up to the rock and then to back off and hang on the edge of the suckhole that results as the wave withdraws a few seconds later. For brief moments, you can surf the wave at the edge of such a temporary hole.

But watch out that you don't get sucked in and spit out,

as Misha Dynnikov did in a giant suckhole on the Mendocino coast. Misha played it for all it was worth as the rest of us watched and photographed—for a while. Then a big wave poured in, and as it passed, Misha got sucked in like a hapless spaceship into a black hole. Fortunately, another wave soon arrived and flushed him back out of that deep trouble spot. That was the day Misha showed us he could roll his Tsunami X-7 in violent turbulence, vault off the bottom, bail out, swim, recover his boat, remount, and paddle like a madman—all in 30 seconds of glory.

Washovers and Cascades

Washovers and *cascades* occur where waves wash over a ledge and pour down into a depression in the rocks. A washover is sloped, like a chute in a river, whereas a cascade is steep, like a waterfall. The Tsunami Rangers' video *Kayaking Ocean Rock Gardens* showcases a dramatic washover on the southern Oregon coast, which we named Dreamer Ridge (see chapter 11, "Resources").

Paddling up to the shoreward edge of a washover or cascade, where an oncoming wave has to roll over the rock before reaching you, is usually a relatively safe move. Even though this phenomenon appears spectacular at close range, most of the wave's energy has been expended by the time it reaches this side of the rock. To avoid colli-sion, a group of kayakers, even if they plan to remain on this leeward side of a washover rock, should fan out and remain parallel to each other.

Attempting to surf *over* a washover or cascade is a much more dangerous and technically demanding maneuver. Judgment and timing are especially critical here. To do so, paddle around to the exposed side of the rock and turn to face it. Once a wave arrives, you are committed to going for it, like a cowboy on a bull when the gate opens. As you begin to hurtle forward, brace far back into the wave to keep your bow up and prevent you from pitch-poling forward. If the maneuver is performed properly, you will clear the edge of the rock and slide smoothly across on a cushion of water. Now get ready for the free fall at the end of your wild ride. Surfing the falls of a cascade or a washover is one of the ultimate rock garden thrills but should only be attempted by an expert rock garden paddler with other experienced team members nearby to assist if anything goes wrong.

Reflecto Zones

At Garrapata, just north of Big Sur, a beautiful *reflecto zone* awaits sea kayakers looking for excitement. Here, waves roll and slam into a vertical cliff face and then reflect back and collide with other waves

Jim Kakuk zooming off a cascade.

John Nagle

John Lull rides a cascade.

following behind, creating dramatic *clapotis* (an upsurge caused by colliding waves). To hang out in a re-flecto zone, position yourself just outside the break, faced out to sea to gauge the approaching swells. Oncoming waves will roll underneath you and explode against the cliff, shooting high into the air and shower-

John Lull backs up to a wall in the reflecto zone.

ing the whole area with spray and invigorating negative ions. If you get in just the right place when two waves come together, you will be thrown skyward by the powerful upsurge. You can also surf the reflecting waves that rebound off the cliff. This is great fun for expert kayakers who place themselves just perfectly so they don't get slammed into the cliff.

Refracto Zones

Waves that rebound off a cliff face are called *reflectos* by rock garden aficionados. When a wave is split by a rock or a reef, and the two sections roll around to meet again, this is referred to as a *refracto zone*. When a divided refracto wave reconverges at an angle, it is known as *convergence*, or a *zipper*, since it looks like a huge zipper being fastened for a few meters or the length of a football field. Refracto zones, such as the one at Flat Rock on the San Mateo coast, generally work best at medium-low tide. Paddlers should therefore be prepared for shallow water and lots of exposed rock as well.

One exciting move in a refracto zone is to position yourself to surf a wave wrapping around a rock right into the other wrapping wave coming from the other side of the rock. If you time it right, the clapotis created by the convergence may pop you high into the air. Surfing in refracto zones is one of the most thrilling ocean whitewater activities.

The Churn That Burns

A *churn*, where a U- or V-shaped rock chute traps and intensifies the energy of breaking waves, can be the ultimate rock garden terror spot. Some churns have no rear exit, and a hapless kayaker caught inside by big waves may have a difficult time escaping. Before paddling into a churn, scout it out and make sure there's a climbable wall or some other escape route if you get trapped.

Eric Soares and a student back into a cauldron.

A *punch bowl* is a churn where a narrow or shallow entrance reduces the wave action inside. In a punch bowl, waves squeeze through the opening and then rebound around the bowl. Once you've dashed through that narrow entrance channel, a punch bowl can be a comparatively benign place to bounce around and enhance your paddling skills.

Wedges, cauldrons, and slits are all varieties of microchurns. A *wedge* is a V-shaped crack in the rocks through which waves may spurt high in the air when they reach the end. A *cauldron* is a small U-shaped churn, perhaps with several subterranean channels leading out to the sea. Waves wash in through the channels and then surge to the surface in a roiling boil. It can be challenging just to remain upright in such a maelstrom. A *slit* is a long, narrow churn that can be especially dangerous when big waves are rolling in. In the Rangers' first video, *The Adventures of the Tsunami Rangers*, Captain Jim Kakuk is shown surfing his Tsunami X-1 Rocket Boat straight into Sniveler's Slit (see chapter 11, "Resources"). The bow of his boat dove to the bottom, causing him to pitch-pole face first right into the rock wall. After that, it was years before anyone tried paddling there again.

Churns are fascinating to observe in action but are probably the most dangerous of all rock garden play spots. Again, only the most skilled rock garden paddlers should attempt paddling there, and then only in moderate conditions. The only place more perilous than a churn when the surf is big is a sea cave, the topic of chapter 8.

> "Break, break, break,
> on thy cold grey stones, O Sea
> Break, break, break,
> at the foot of the crags, O Sea."
>
> —Alfred Lord Tennyson, 1875

8 Sea Caves

> " A wave in a cave is grave. "
>
> —Diego Cienfuegos

Sea caves are dark and potentially dangerous places, but human beings are still fascinated by them. Since ancient times, adventurers, pirates, and mystics have sought out places where caves opened to the sea. Myths and legends from many cultures have referred to these mysterious caverns as entrances to the womb of Mother Earth and the habitat of assorted nymphs, sirens, sibyls, and demons who jealously guarded magical pools brimming with the power of eternal life and who lured hapless sailors to their doom. In a sea cave's bowels, one could expect to meet Tolkien's Gothmog the balrog or perhaps encounter a baleful dragon who could only be slain by a great hero like Beowulf.

The ability of sea kayakers to navigate rugged stretches of shoreline up close have enabled them access to many remote and previously unexplored sea caves along the Pacific coast of North America and elsewhere in the world. Actually paddling into caves can be scary, especially caves exposed to the effects of powerful surf and currents. But the rich smells and echoing sounds, the shimmering pastel colors and interplay of shadow and light, and the continually changing ambiance of these otherworldly places make them irresistible.

Memorable caves inspire colorful names, such as Wizard's Tube, the Green Room, Pirate's Labyrinth, Sniveler's

Every evening Cathedral Cove is filled with light and waves from an arch and two tunnels.

Shaft, the Gilchrist Rhomboid, Trilogy Cathedral, the Black Hole, and the Cave That Ate Dave. Stories abound of unforgettable and sometimes hair-raising paddling adventures in sea caves. Kayakers have gotten disoriented while meandering through underground labyrinths, chanced upon cathedral rooms where hidden beaches served as rookeries for harbor seals, and floated over pools deep within sea caves filled with turquoise light emanating from underwater channels.

To help make your forays into sea caves as safe as possible, we share here what we and others have learned about cave features, hazards, and rescue procedures. But first, a caveat: sea caves where waves are present can be as deadly as they are beautiful. Inexperienced paddlers should never enter a sea cave where surging seas are present. This is a realm for expert kayakers only, and they should attempt it only as a team.

The Fourth Dimension

To convey the danger and excitement of sea caves, it's useful to describe sea conditions in four dimensions of ever increasing intensity. The First Dimension is the normal sea state, that is, the open water with gentle wind and waves. The Second Dimension is the surf zone, where a new factor enters the equation—ocean swells colliding with an ocean floor. Rock gardens comprise the Third Dimension, where that sea floor grows irregular and rocks thrust to the surface to further intensify the wave action. Sea caves, with their ceilings, constrictions, and darkness, make up the Fourth Dimension, where danger increases geometrically. Sea caves earn 20 points on the SCRS because they are so deceptively dangerous. Combine a sea cave with surf and rocks, and you get risk thrice compounded.

Types of Sea Caves

Let's explore the different types of caves and their attributes. Sea caves occur when wave and surge action carves out a section of weaker rock, usually along a fault. Most of the sea caves the Rangers and other paddlers have encountered in California, Hawaii, and Oregon are volcanic, although some have been carved in granite, sandstone, siltstone, or a combination of these rocks. No one we know has yet explored a limestone sea cave, though they probably exist on coasts somewhere in the world.

The National Speleological Society has its own way of labeling cave types. David Bunnell's interesting and instructive book, *Sea Caves of Santa Cruz Island*, identifies types of sea caves and includes a comprehensive method of charting caves (see chapter 11, "Resources"). This book is recommended for anyone seriously contemplating sea cave exploration.

The Tsunami Rangers have developed a more fanciful way of classifying caves. A small, narrow cave, shallow and straight, is called a *shaft*. A shaft often has a geometric-shaped opening, such as a rhomboid shape. A *tube* is a long, narrow tunnel that often bends and narrows as it leads inward. A *cavern* is a cave with a big room and a high ceiling. A complex cave with caverns and many passages and rooms is called a *labyrinth* or *maze*. A cavern with majestic light shining down from above is a *cathedral*, and an elaborate cavern is referred to as a *grotto*.

Sea Cave Features

Though similar in some ways, each cave has unique features. It is helpful for kayakers to categorize them. The *dripline* is the official name for the opening of a cave (it's where rainwater would drip down from the entrance). An *exit* or *side door* is a way that water flows out of a cave, and the *rear* is the back end of a cave. A *tooth* is a rock like a stalactite or stalagmite. If the tooth is pointy, it's a *canine*; if it's mostly flat, it's a *molar*.

An *elevator* is a rapid rise and fall of surge in a cave. It usually occurs in conjunction with a *squeeze*, a very narrow or enclosed section, where water is constricted in a sea cave. The opposite of a squeeze is a *room*, with a high ceiling and widely spaced walls, where the elevator effects of surging water are less. Usually a room is a good place for a *station*, a relatively safe place when surge or breaking waves come through. Typically, surges occur in wider caves with deep water, and waves break in narrower passages or where water is more shallow.

Mapping a Sea Cave

Charts and topographical maps don't often indicate sea caves. Only a few dedicated sea cave explorers such as Bunnell have mapped marine caves, and only a few areas, such as the Channel

In the Lair of the Balrog

Back in 1986, Eric, Dave Whalen, Bill Collins, and I were exploring caves on the Oregon coast. One day we came upon a cave that looked like a dragon's lair, partially obscured by a waterfall scrim. Somebody promptly named it Veil Cave. For a while we peered through the mists that swirled around the entrance of the cave, but we couldn't see much. Finally, I sent Eric in to probe.

Eric reemerged a few minutes later to report that the cave was a uniform tube about 40 feet in diameter that went back about 200 feet and then turned east under the mountains. This diminished the chances of there being another opening, unless it was into Hell itself. More than 300 feet of solid rock towered above, with ocean below. Eric suggested that we explore deeper.

Since Dave and Bill were relatively inexperienced, we set them up as scouts outside the cave. Eric and I slipped through the waterfall and continued paddling until we reached the place where the cave turned east. We paused here a while to let our eyes grow accustomed to the darkness. Then we spun our boats around and began backing farther into the cave. In this way we could keep an eye on the waves rolling in from the entrance. By turning our heads, we could also dimly see the waves moving deeper down the corridor behind us. We allowed the waves to push us gently backward for about 150 feet, and then we paused while I took some pictures. There was barely enough light, but I snapped away at Eric silhouetted against the eerie scene.

A shout caused us to glance toward the entrance, where Dave was signaling wildly, "Big waves!" I stowed the camera under my PFD (also known as "photographer's flak diverter") and prepared to meet the onslaught.

As a wave rose to nearly fill the mouth of the cave, I thought, "The giant sea worm's going to swallow us." I noticed there was still a little head room above the not-quite-breaking wave, so I thought we would be okay.

The wave grew in strength as it rapidly closed the gap between us, and it filled the cave with a sound like a locomotive in a tunnel. We dropped into a trough just before the wave hit. I felt I was in a pit with Maleficent the dragon. I heard Eric yell, "We can make it." Ha.

I dug in with my paddle to maintain my position. Everything went into fast motion as the wave lifted us toward the ceiling. The bow of Eric's boat banged into mine and halted my forward motion. The wave drove me back another 20 feet farther into the twilight zone and up against the side of the cave, like a skateboarder careening backward through a cement culvert. Then the wave rounded the corner and continued on, into the abyss. The last sounds I heard were a rumble and a deep moan as the balrog engulfed the wave.

Eric shouted, "Let's get . . . !" but I was already on my way. We rode the backwash out to get a head start on the next wave.

(continued on page 89)

Islands off southern California, have been studied. Generally, the only way to learn about sea caves is to explore them yourself. Few sea kayakers take the time to map caves, although they love to name them and to describe to each other the ones they've explored. The map of Shipwreck Cave in Santa Cruz Island illustrates how a sea cave should be mapped.

Cave Hazards

Even though a sea cave may seem intriguing, you should never just impulsively paddle into one. Particularly on an exposed coast, a significant surge or a big wave could arrive, even when the open sea is calm.

More than any other time in the ocean, wearing a helmet is essential when paddling in sea caves. In the darkness it might be easy to overlook a low ceiling, and the water level and overhead clearance in a cave where surge is present can change abruptly. You could also strike your partners with a paddle blade or run into them with your boat in the close quarters encountered in a sea cave.

Narrow passages can be tricky because you could get wedged, and, of course, a surge at that moment could add to your trouble. Where powerful currents or surge is running through a cave, the danger of getting stuck in a rock sieve also exists. Stalactites, stalagmites, or debris jammed in a cave are also potential threats. A rare, but formidable, hazard in a cave occurs when a wave or littoral current flows under a ledge, which may suck an unwary boater underwater.

A breaking wave in a cave is probably the worst danger a sea kayaker will encounter, the epitome of the Fourth Dimension.

Waves in caves get compressed and rise up toward the ceiling with tremendous force. This occurs commonly in caves that face the open sea. Also, sometimes waves roll into a cave from two or more entrances and meet inside, creating additional havoc.

During the making of the video *The Adventures of the Tsunami Rangers*, a waterproof movie camera was bolted to the foredeck of Michael's kayak when Jim Kakuk and the authors paddled into a sea cave near Point Bonita (see chapter 11, "Resources"). A big wave roared in, and the entire tube filled to the ceiling with breaking water. Boats collided with each other, and helmets and paddle blades glanced off rocks, but everyone escaped from the cave unscathed. Watch the video to get the full effect of this scene as it unfolded, and you may think twice before casually paddling into a sea cave.

How to Remain Safe and Have Fun in Sea Caves

Read chapter 2 for information on lights and rescue equipment appropriate for sea cave penetration. For safety and identification, each person should wear a different-colored chemical light stick on the back of his or her helmet. Pack along an extra light or two, such as a portable diver's flashlight, in case your primary light fails or gets lost

(continued from page 88)

We cleared it with an adrenaline burst and exited the sea serpent's maw with lightning flickering off our fingers. It felt good to be back in the warmth of the sun.

Now I understand why sailors in the old days believed that dragons and demons hung out in caves. Sometimes at night, I recall Veil Cave and dream about returning there. Someday, we sea trogs will boogie with the balrogs again.

—Jim Kakuk

deep inside a cave. If you anticipate facing breaking waves, you may wish to wear pads on your shoulders, elbows, knees, and shins. Eric often takes fins along, so he can swim out of a cave if his boat gets disabled. If you plan to survey a cave, you will find useful a diver's slate for recording data, a diver's wrist compass, and survey tape.

A floating throw bag with a light stick attached to the bag should be kept accessible on each person's deck. Quick-release D-rings, snap shackles, or carabiners kept on both ends of a rescue line make clipping onto a boat or the front of a paddler's PFD quick and easy.

Certain procedures and skills can maximize fun and mitigate hazards. Begin by always scouting a cave from outside before entering. Observe what happens as the biggest waves of a set hit. Even if you can't see what is happening inside the cave, the sounds that breaking

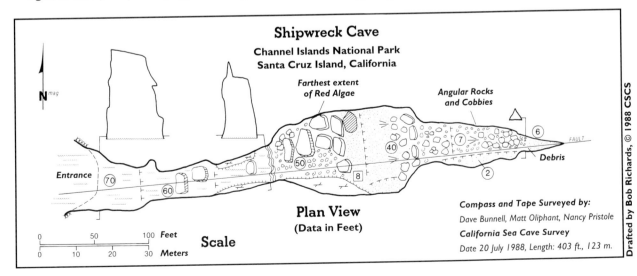

Shipwreck Cave
Channel Islands National Park
Santa Cruz Island, California

Farthest extent of Red Algae

Angular Rocks and Cobbies

N mag

FAULT

Debris

Entrance

Plan View
(Data in Feet)

0   50   100 Feet
0 10 20 30 Meters   **Scale**

Compass and Tape Surveyed by:
Dave Bunnell, Matt Oliphant, Nancy Pristole
California Sea Cave Survey
Date 20 July 1988, Length: 403 ft., 123 m.

Drafted by Bob Richards, © 1988 CSCS

waves make after they roll through the entrance can reveal how deep a cave is and what's happening inside. A succession of loud booming sounds echoing back to the scouts outside may be enough to warn them not to paddle into a particular cave. If a big wave goes through and produces hardly any sound at all, the water is not being restricted much nor being forced into breaking. Instead, it is either rushing through and out another opening, or the cave is much wider inside than at the opening and may have a sandy beach at the back upon which the waves are gently lapping.

Typically, caves are more hazardous in the winter months when the weather intensifies. This is certainly true on the Pacific coasts of both North and South America, when increased storm activity is more likely to push huge swells ashore. Low tide is safer for caves with low ceilings or hanging teeth; a higher tide is generally best in caves with high ceilings and rocky, irregular floors. These are generalizations, not hard and fast rules, since conditions vary.

Remember, you are safer operating in a cave as a team. A good leader will assign the other paddlers specific roles and responsibilities in case of an emergency. The leader directs an experienced cave boater to go in alone and probe. The solo paddler ventures in only as far as is possible in the natural light and then returns quickly to report any hazards and describe where safe zones are situated. If the cave

seems safe to explore, a penetration plan is devised, with at least one person remaining outside the mouth of the cave to watch the sea and signal a warning if a large set of waves is seen approaching. If the cave is deep, another boater may remain just inside the dripline to pass along messages from the outside scout. If you have at least five members in your team, and the cave veers in a different direction, you may wish to position another scout at station near the turn and in sight of the dripline scout.

The most experienced paddlers lead the team deeper into the cave. They stay side by side, not stacked up, and remain in contact with the signal boaters, in case a big wave comes rolling in. If the cave is narrow, one paddler pauses at a deep station while the other probes for the next soft spot. Paddlers with washdeck boats may slip off, swim around, and explore, especially in a narrow cave with a low ceiling.

In a sea cave where waves are present, keep the bows of the boats pointing toward the cave entrance and any sizable waves that should roll in. This makes a quick escape possible, should a big set arrive. It's a bad idea to allow a boat to get perpendicular in a narrow cave, as this invites wedging. The team should remain in contact with each other and communicate with a combination of vocal, light, and hand signals (see chapter 9 for a complete list of hand signals). If the group happens upon a big and relatively safe cavern, like Painted Cave on Santa Cruz Island, then the entrance scouts and less experienced paddlers can enter and join in the fun.

Cave Rescues

What if you, or a person in your team, needs help while kayaking in a sea cave? First off, forget about assistance from the Coast Guard or any other rescue agencies. They would be unable to reach you, crammed in a crevice a few hundred feet inside a mountainside with sea water gushing in and out. You and your team members must be prepared to rescue yourselves. It is a time for clear thinking and decisive action, not a time to whimper. Here are a few situations you might encounter, with some practical ways to help yourself.

Misha Dynnikov, at station, waits for Eric to enter the cave.

If you get pushed up against the ceiling by elevating water, the safest thing to do is to roll over quickly and allow the hull to take the impact. Roll back up or swim over and remount when the surge goes down; then paddle out before another wave surges in. In especially chaotic conditions, where collision with both the floor and ceiling are possible, a paddler may be better off remaining in the water, scrambling atop the boat each time the water withdraws and ducking underneath it again when another surge pushes it back toward the ceiling. Then swim or paddle out, as soon as things settle down again.

Each time a big wave comes in, either duck into a protected area until the wave passes, or paddle straight into the oncoming wave and punch through it to exit the cave. If the wave hits you hard and capsizes you, try to roll or vault back up quickly; then resume your efforts to get out of the cave or reach a soft spot.

Should a breaking wave begin surfing you toward the back of a cave, first lean and brace deeply into the wave to avoid capsizing. Stay calm and exercise the paddling techniques you learned in the surf zone to maintain control. Like any surf, there are moments of respite between waves and sets when you can regain control and escape. If all else fails, you may have to temporarily abandon your boat and swim out of a cave.

If you have lost your boat and are having trouble swimming out of the cave, don't wait until you are exhausted and panicked; instead, immediately yell for help. Should a companion throw you a rope or throw bag, grab it and start swimming toward the boat, or hold onto the rope and frog kick if the rescue boat is heading toward the exit. If a boater or swimmer approaches to help you, remain calm and do as the rescuer instructs.

A Surreal Moment While Filming in a Cave

When National Geographic Explorer asked the Tsunami Rangers to help them make a show for national television about extreme-condition sea kayaking in January of 1993, we were excited. We never anticipated, however, that for the sea cave sequence, the film crew would ask us to pack airplane batteries inside the hatches of our kayaks and attach high-intensity underwater lights to the bows of our crafts. But that's exactly what they did.

Big winter storm swells were hammering California as we led the National Geographic film crew to one of our favorite paddling destinations, deep in Big Sur. Pirate's Labyrinth, as we called it, was a spectacular stretch of coastline where dozens of sea caves riddled the bases of the mountains spilling abruptly down into the sea. After rappelling down cliffs to the sea, we loaded the heavy batteries into the front hatches of our washdeck boats and taped the lights to our bows. The only problem was that those lights were designed to operate underwater and would quickly overheat above the surface. To keep them cool long enough to shoot the scene, we were instructed to continually splash water on them with our paddles, once we turned them on.

Jim Kakuk, Maura Kistler, and I paddled into a sea cave in single boats, followed by Eric and filmmaker Gordon Brown in a Tsunami X-2 double kayak. Michael Brown, Gordon's brother, swam in holding a second waterproof movie camera. We switched on the lights, and for a few minutes everything went according to plan.

Then a set of powerful waves began rolling in, and the interior of the grotto was immediately transformed into a gigantic blender. The roar of the whitewater and the whoops of the paddlers reverberated off the rocky walls and became an incomprehensible cacophony. In the ensuing melee, the paddlers promptly forgot about splashing water on the lights, which soon overheated and began smoking. Through the swirling smoke and whitewater chaos, I caught glimpses of the Brown brothers, both in the water now with their cameras, shooting and trying to stay out of the way of the wildly rebounding kayaks. Then, one by one, the superheated lights began exploding. The overall effect was quite surreal, like a scene out of a bizarre Dantesque comedy. We all raced back into the brilliant sunshine, gasping for air and nearly falling out of our boats with laughter.

—Michael

Dark Incident in a Sea Cave

My wife Nani and I stopped one day at Van Damme State Beach on the scenic Mendocino coast in northern California. The sea appeared calm, and we decided to go kayaking along the rocky, convoluted shoreline that stretched out beyond the beach. Since our original intention was to paddle only in open water, not to surf or explore rock gardens, we didn't wear our whitewater helmets.

We had only gone a little way when we came to the entrance of a sea cave. On closer inspection we realized it was actually a long tunnel that led through the rocks to another opening, facing the open sea.

I asked Nani to wait outside the entrance to the tunnel cave while I checked it out. The water was reassuringly tranquil in the protected cove where we paddled, and it felt safe. The action of the surf out beyond the front entrance was sending small waves undulating through the tunnel, and for a few moments it was magical. Nani paddled in to join me.

Just then, however, a set of bigger waves began to hit at the front entrance. Compressing as it came through the tunnel, the first wave raced toward us until it was nearly as high as our heads. I reflexively dug in with my paddle to punch through and yelled to Nani, who was less experienced, to do the same. She made it through the wave but ended up right up against the cave wall, a bad place to be. The next wave caught her and surfed her backward toward me. The stern of her little slalom kayak snowplowed deep into the water, and she catapulted over backward. She came down, face first, right on the deck of my boat. Unfortunately, that is where I had mounted a metal bracket for waterproof cameras.

Nani and her boat splashed into the water beside me after impact, upside down. I grabbed her and rolled her back up, but her spray skirt had popped loose, and she was half out of her boat. Luckily, the wave action had washed us back out the rear entrance of the tunnel cave by now. Nani was pretty shook up, but with me beside her she was able to paddle back to shore. The first thing she did after we landed was put her hand to her mouth and make sure her teeth were all still there. We were grateful, too, that her jaw was not broken, although it was mighty sore for a few days.

We learned some important lessons that day. First, we would never paddle anywhere near surf and rocks again without our helmets. We had experienced, close up, how suddenly and dramatically things can change around the ocean. We also were reminded how important it is to possess advanced surf and rock garden skills before paddling into sea caves. They are extraordinarily beautiful, sacred places, but it is dangerous to venture into them unprepared.

—*Michael*

Michael Powers surfs out of a labyrinth.

Eric Soares

If no one can help you, do not panic. Keep your wits about you and calmly swim out of the cave. Never surrender to the siren's voice telling you to give up.

If you see a paddling companion in trouble, and you are safe at station, first attempt to help by offering verbal suggestions or throwing a tow rope. Don't get close unless absolutely necessary. Why? Because if you risk also becoming trapped or capsized in a cave situation, it can make things much worse. If you determine, however, that a victim is unable to get out of trouble without assistance, remain calm, reassuring, and decisive. Once you have committed to rescue someone, it is imperative to take total control of the situation. A "rescue attempt" is an oxymoron.

Unless the victim is disabled or panicked, the offering of a tow rope or the stern of your boat to hold onto may suffice. If you and the victim are both swimming, and the swimmer is conscious, *never* grab him or let her grab you because you could be drowned as the victim claws at your body to stay afloat. Instead of your hand, extend a rescue tube, a rope, or your paddle to the victim. If nothing else is available, and you are an excellent swimmer, remove your PFD and hand one end of it to the victim. Then you can swim and tow the victim to safety without being grabbed by the victim.

An unconscious victim is certainly a serious matter, but less of a threat to your own personal safety. If you are swimming, spin the unconscious victim around so his back is facing you. Place your right arm under the victim's right armpit and across the upper chest. Grab the left front of his or her PFD, the left armpit, or the left shoulder. Make sure the victim's head is above water. Then swim to your boat or the entrance, using the sidestroke. If the victim is

A kayaker paddles hard to gain momentum to avoid being driven backward in a sea cave.

Allegory of the Sea Cave

In Plato's "Allegory of the Cave," a man climbs out of the hole of limited knowledge and discovers the light of the sun. Indeed, the sun gives us power, enabling us to develop our marvelous civilizations and technology. But perhaps, from time to time, we need to be reminded of our humble origins, when we found comfort and safety in the darkness of caves. Paddling sea kayaks along the edge of the sea is a way back to the world of our ancestors.

Exploring sea caves is, without question, one of the pinnacle experiences of extreme-condition sea kayaking. It can be practiced in reasonable safety by first developing solid surf and rock garden skills and then by remaining conscious of the special circumstances present in sea caves as discussed in this chapter. Finally, *always* exercise good judgment when exploring sea caves. Go with a team, and seek solace and adventure through those wondrous openings into the hidden realm where the earth envelopes the sea. You may come face to face with a siren, a dragon, or a deeper dimension of yourself.

Dave Whalen, in a contemplative mood.

floating, place your cupped right hand under the chin (instead of under the armpit and across the chest), pull the victim's head back, and swim out using the sidestroke. This method is faster and less tiring for the rescuer. If your swim fins are handy, quickly don them before beginning the rescue; they will make your kicks much more powerful. Once you are back in your boat, grab the person by the top of the PFD, heave the victim face down across your lap, and paddle out of the cave. Hail your companions for assistance. Get to a beach quickly and administer CPR or other first aid as needed.

These rescues seem extreme, and they are. But, of course, an ounce of prudence is worth a pound of rescue. Be mindful that these same techniques also work in rock gardens, surf, and the open sea. Both the authors have saved people in imminent danger of drowning and have faced other semicritical rescue situations that occurred in extreme sea conditions. We hope that you will never have to rescue anyone, but if you intend to paddle a kayak in extreme conditions, it's definitely wise to practice these procedures and be prepared. Otherwise, you would be better off exploring the pool at the Mirage Hotel in Las Vegas.

Power of the Tribe

> " We all have one thing in common. We don't want to die. "
>
> —Commander Eric Soares, Tsunami Rangers

Audrey Sutherland's "Go simple, go solo, go now" credo rings true for many who feel drawn to Poseidon's playground. Some are individualists who view sea kayaking as an escape from conformity. They envision themselves alone in a boat, exploring vast expanses of oceanic frontier. This yearning for isolation is intensified by the pressure of the benighted, technological society that surrounds us. In addition, wandering in cyberspace, watching television, driving on freeways, and many other modern activities allow us to get by without much personal interaction. So conditioned, we tend to romanticize escaping into the sea alone. But when actually plying the waters solo, our psyches may whisper: "It's lonely, and a little scary out here. Perhaps sea kayaking would be safer and more enjoyable in the company of others. Who are my people? Where is *my sea tribe?*"

So, consciously or unconsciously, we seek like-minded individuals to share our passion for adventure in the sea. We visit kayak shops, show up at kayak regattas and symposia, check out a local kayak club, respond to group paddling opportunities. In time, as we meet the right people, we form a kayaking group, or even a team, the modern version of a sea tribe.

Members of a kayak team line up parallel to each other to maintain communication and avoid collision.

Unified Purpose

Sea kayakers have long demonstrated their capacity to travel far and wide alone. Consider the epic solo paddling journeys of Audrey Sutherland along the coasts of Hawaii and southeast Alaska, or Ed

Gillet, who kayaked across the vast Pacific to Hawaii. Yet for most of us, paddling with others provides camaraderie, a greater margin of safety, and the opportunity to learn from one another and to share the wonder of exploring the marine environment. A lone kayaker naturally tends to err on the side of caution; a team feels empowered to take calculated risks. Camping for a soloist is a solitary bivouac; for team members it can be a time of festive celebration and storytelling around the fire.

Elite military units subscribe to a concept called *unit integrity*, whereby squad members are enabled to function together, smoothly and as a cohesive unit. Richard Marcinko, a navy SEAL commando, stated, "The single most important element in creating a battle-ready special-ops force is unit integrity. Unit integrity means your men think and act in concert, each supporting the others." For paddlers also, a common purpose or goal has long helped everyone to realize full benefit from a team. For the ancient sea tribes, unit integrity was essential. Aleuts and Inuits discovered that by forming hunting parties, they could pursue whales, seals, and other game more safely and effectively. Today, an integrated team may work together to explore and chart an unfamiliar coast, fish or forage for food, execute a risky rock garden stunt, or capture the adventure of sea kayaking in extreme conditions on film.

The Tsunami Rangers raft up to hold a strategy meeting before entering a rock garden.

pool their individual efforts to enjoy the benefits and synergism denied to lone paddlers.

Since prehistoric times, humans have worked together to survive and achieve their goals, from aboriginal hunting parties to astronauts exploring space. Modern society abounds with teams: surgical units, marching bands, roofers, football teams. Successful teamwork requires solid structure, effective communication, complemental tasks, and agreement on unified action. A good kayak team invariably incorporates these factors.

Paddling Groups, Teams, and Clubs

A sea kayak *club* is a group of folks who meet regularly to socialize, share knowledge and information of specific interest to ocean paddlers, and organize trips and activities. *Sea Kayaker* magazine lists well over 100 kayak clubs around the world. A *team* may strive to accomplish many of the objectives of a club but is generally smaller, less formally organized, and more focused on a particular style of paddling. But just as with a club, team members

Groups versus Teams

The Tsunami Rangers consider themselves a kayaking *team*, as opposed to a group. Commander John Lull has determined in which ways teams differ from groups. He points out that in a kayaking team, each individual strives to achieve self sufficiency and adequate skill levels while still functioning in a coordinated fashion. Team members develop methods of communicating, sometimes quite specialized, that enable them to respond quickly and effectively to common needs, especially in perilous circumstances. They work to support and complement each other, which enables everyone to develop their paddling skills and push their limits much further than they would ever dare to do alone.

In a casual paddling group, however, members may or may not be skilled and self-sufficient, and the weaker paddlers might have to rely heavily upon the others for guidance and well-being. The goals of individuals within the group may be different, and everyone is not necessarily aware of each other's strengths and weaknesses. Communication between the kayakers is disorganized and could break down completely in extreme conditions.

Dynamics of Team Paddling

The feeling that each member can trust his or her companions explicitly, even in the most precarious of circumstances, is one of the great rewards of unit integrity. Ideally, individual strengths will offset weaknesses within a team, as members contribute what they can to the common good.

We have discovered that on the water, three paddlers often make an optimum team. Decision making is quicker, and if one person gets in trouble, two can often help better than one. An even number has an advantage of pairing people up into dyads and using a buddy system, where the two paddlers watch each other's backs. A larger assemblage tends to become unwieldy when a big wave rolls in or things otherwise start to get wild. When six or more team members gather for a Tsunami mission, we sometimes break up into two or more squads, based on complemental skills and mutual interests, which makes decision making and communication easier in extreme conditions. We may not regroup until back in protected water or around the campfire at night.

We have adapted the traditional naval system of ranking members for our own use. Rank is assigned to members based upon paddling skill and experience, ancillary skills, judgment, leadership qualities, initiative, and knowledge of the sea environment. Higher rank implies a greater responsibility for directing team activities and ensuring safety. The most senior ranking officer in the Tsunami Rangers is Captain Jim Kakuk.

Following in seniority are commanders, lieutenant commanders, lieutenants, and so on. A commander's role is often to find and explore new stretches of coast, lead team missions, and act as probe when things appear particularly intimidating. Lower-ranking Rangers also participate fully in extreme sea kayaking adventures but are not expected to assume leadership positions or as great a degree of responsibility for the safety of others.

Complemental Tasks

When members of the Tsunami Ranger team prepare to go out kayaking, we are inclined to say, "We're going on a mission." The mission might be probing a newly discovered sea cave or rock garden, photographing each other paddling through a spectacular marine environment, or exploring a wilderness coast. On these missions, each team member has specific responsibilities. For example, as mentioned in chapter 8, when we enter an unknown cave, the captain will assign roles to team members. One kayaker remains outside to watch out for big waves, another pauses just inside to relay information, a third kayaker may take up position where a corridor makes a turn, while the most experienced paddler, probably a commander, penetrates to the deepest recesses of the cavern. Operating in this fashion, we are able to paddle in areas that could be dangerous to an individual or unorganized group.

The complemental style of paddling becomes important when an extreme-condition kayaking team decides to move out along an exposed coast in rough conditions. When the sea is calm, everyone relaxes and paddles in a random shotgun pattern, enjoying the unfolding view. But when the wind and waves kick up, we fall into *formation*, where each person takes up a position that best serves the needs of the team. This formation can take different forms, depending on sea conditions, team size, and skill levels. When heading into a strong wind, a tight *column* formation may be employed so the following paddlers can draft off the lead boat. In following seas, kayakers spread out into a broad row formation to stay out of each other's way. When the wind is abeam, an *inverted-V* formation serves to keep everyone in range for visual communication.

A team paddles in formation while negotiating a kelp garden.

Imagine a six-person team moving down an exposed coast in an *inverted-V arrow* formation. The boat in *point* or *lead* position is a strong kayaker who is experienced at piloting and maintaining a steady pace that everyone can follow.

low. The two boaters on the side points of the arrowhead are scouts who are available to check out landing sites and other points of interest. The side-point boaters also ride herd on the middle positions in the arrow's shaft, occupied by the two weakest or most heavily laden paddlers. The boat at the bottom of the arrow shaft is in the *sweep* or *control* position, the best place to observe, assist, and communicate with other team members, so the team leader takes this position.

Communication

Precise, clear, audible and visual signals are essential to a sea paddling team. Some kayak guides and trip leaders carry whistles tethered to their PFDs. The Tsunami Rangers commonly employ a distinctive, high-pitched vocal signal to capture each other's attention: "HOYT!" Once the attention of other team members has been obtained, the Ranger wishing to communicate will follow with one or a succession of visual signals. The others also respond visually and then act or relay the message. Most of these visual signals were devised to require only one hand, leaving the other hand free to grasp the paddle and control the boat.

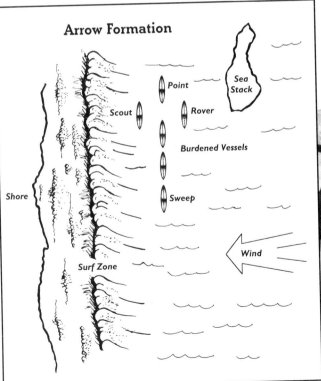

Arrow Formation

Sea Stack

Point

Scout

Rover

Burdened Vessels

Shore

Sweep

Wind

Surf Zone

D. Volturno

Eric Soares shows the futility of a cell phone conversation in the surf.

Signal Grammar

To save time and avoid confusion during on-the-water communication, sentence structure is kept simple (subject/predicate/object), and only active voice is employed. Just nouns, verbs, and adjectives are generally used, and the same pronouns suffice for both subjective and objective situations. A typical hand signal statement might go, "YOU COME I," which means, "Please come over here and join me." Other sentences could indicate the intention to take personal action ("I PHOTOGRAPH"), convey a mood or describe something ("THIS IS SCARY!"), or ask a question ("YOU OKAY?").

SCOUT (go scout that)

SCARY! (looks wild and scary!)

HANG (wait here for me)

BAD (that's a bad idea)

BORING (it's boring)

CUT (let's quit)

Tsunami Ranger Hand Signals

TERM	HOW SIGNALED	MEANING
Nouns		
I/ME	Point index finger toward self	Yourself
IT/THEM	Point index finger toward object	Object, place, people
YOU	Point index finger toward person(s)	Person(s)
WE/US	Point index finger at group and circle	All of us
Verbs		
COME	Beckon with index finger	Come here
CUT	Bring index finger across throat	Let's quit
FORM UP	Circle index finger above head	Gather around
GET CLOSE	Thumb held close to index finger	Get in close
GO	Hold forearm horizontally and revolve as if winding string on a spool	Go forward or backward
GROK	Tap bunched up fingers on temple	Pay attention
HANG	Shoot arm straight out with palm down	Wait here a while
IGNORE	Throw air over shoulder	Ignore my last signal
LAND	Bring hand down, palm down	Head to shore and land
LEAD	Bring hand to forehead and make a salute	Advance to front/lead the group
RAFT UP	Tap clenched fist on paddle shaft	Raft up and confer
RELAX	Lower hand slowly, palm down	Relax
SCOUT	Hold horizontal hand over brow	Scout the way I'm facing
SPREAD	Hold fist near head and then spread fingers	Fan out
STAY AWAY	Move hand away from body	Get away from danger
STOP	Put hand in air and close fist	Stop/hold position
SURF	Move hand in snake motion	Surf and play
SWEEP	Move hand in sweeping motion	Fall behind group and sweep
WAIT	Hold index finger up near head	Wait a moment
Descriptors		
BAD	Thumb down	Bad idea or move
BORING	Pat yawning mouth with palm	Boring/uninteresting
DANGEROUS	Arm or paddle horizontal over head	Not safe/don't advance
GOOD	Clenched fist with thumb up	Good idea or move
GROOVY	Cross arms or paddles	Impressive move or surf ride
NOT HURT	Pat head with palm	Not hurt/everything is okay
SAFE	Arm or paddle vertical above head	Safe to go
SCARY!	Hand in tiger claw gesture near head	Extremely wild/scary
STUPID	Slap forehead with open hand	Stupid/error
UNCERTAIN	Rotate hand side to side with palm down	Not sure/can't decide/iffy
Miscellaneous Signals		
'BYE	Wave open hand up and down	Good-bye/end transmission
CHICKEN	Flap elbow against side like a wing	Afraid
GOT IT	Form a circle with thumb and index finger	I understand
GREETING	Hand upraised in Vulcan greeting	Salutation of greeting
HAIL	Wave arm or paddle over head	Hail, listen up
HELP!	Wave arm wildly over head	Help! Assistance needed
NO	Shake head side to side	No/I disagree
QUESTION?	Place palm up near shoulder	Wanna?/don't understand
WILL COMPLY	Military salute	I will comply
AFFIRMATIVE	Shake head up and down	Yes/I agree

A Sample Hand Signal Conversation

When to Use Signals

Hand signals should be employed whenever verbal conversation is not possible or appropriate. If verbal communication is desired, whistle or shout to gain attention, and then use the hand signals HAIL and RAFT UP to draw the others close together for verbal communication.

If at night or in caves, use light signals. A light waving side to side means "It is not safe; don't go." A light waving up and down means "It is safe; you can go." A light waving wildly means "Help!"

Remember that hand signals are always expressed in the active voice. Nonverbal inflections can be added to indicate urgency (e.g., horizontally revolving the forearm quickly, to say "GO! GO! GO!"). Use the QUESTION? hand signal if you don't understand what another paddler is signaling to you. Also, the QUESTION? signal can be used to soften a command and make it a request. Suppose one of your paddling companions exits a sea cave. You whistle, point to the cave, and raise your upturned palm to your shoulder to ask "What's happening in the cave?" Your partner also responds with the QUESTION? signal, indicating she did not understand you. You point to the cave and then repeat your QUESTION? signal. Your companion now understands you and responds: SCARY, STAY AWAY, DANGER. She points at both of you, then points toward a nearby surf zone, and concludes with an upturned palm at the shoulder to signal YOU. ME. SURF THERE. WANNA? The QUESTION? signal at the end indicates the communication is an invitation to go surf, not a command.

Signals should be practiced by sea kayaking teams until they have developed the ability to communicate visually even under the most adverse conditions. With enough practice, communicating by hand signals will become reflexive and require little conscious thought.

Training and Development

For an extreme sea kayaking team to function safely and effectively, it must regularly practice hand signals, paddling in formation, group rescues, and advanced techniques. Paddlers with special skills (e.g., diving, photography, wilderness first aid, rock climbing) can share their skills with teammates so everyone receives cross-training in cognate skills. Expert paddlers sponsor and train less experienced ones and keep an eye on trainees when on the water.

The British Canoe Union pioneered the formal testing of kayaking proficiency among student paddlers. We have emulated the BCU by establishing a grueling test combining an oral cross-examination and an on-the-water skill demonstration that cadets take to become an officer (a person wholly responsible for himself or herself on the water). A candidate's knowledge of navigation and hand signals, leadership qualities, paddling skills (ability to Eskimo roll, surf, perform rescues, kayak in rock gardens and caves), and general sea sense are all thoroughly tested. Only after a candidate passes all phases of the entrance test is he or she officially accepted into the Rangers. New Rangers are assigned rank commensurate with the judgment, skill, and leadership qualities they demonstrated during the day-long test.

The Making of a Tsunami Ranger

When stories about the Tsunami Rangers started circulating on the California coast more than a dozen years ago, it stirred up something deep and primal within me. I remember walking along the beach with my Chilean wife, Nani, one day. I exclaimed, "The Tsunami Rangers! They sound like some of my old comic book heroes. I hope to meet these wild men someday." I thought I detected a feeling of dread flicker across my wife's face. Perhaps it was the same look that the loved ones of fisherfolk have worn since time immemorial as they stood vigil on the shore, awaiting the safe return of hunters from the sea. My gaze followed hers, out across the sea to where big waves were breaking like white fangs across a distant reef. Neither of us suspected then that the time would come when I would make my bid to become a Tsunami Ranger.

One day in the fall of 1987, Lady Destiny made her move. Eric Soares, cofounder and a commander of the Tsunami Rangers, landed his sleek X-1 Rocket Boat on the beach in front of our home. Meeting the Tsunami Rangers signified a quantum leap forward for me, into the heady world of extreme-condition sea kayaking. Here was a band of true wave warriors who introduced structure and order, even ritual, into what until then had been merely my halting solitary response to the call of the sea.

Eric and the other Rangers soon taught me hand signals that enabled me to communicate with them at a distance or when the roar of the sea and the wind swept our words away. They led me into sea caves and rock-strewn surf zones, places where I would never dream of paddling alone. It was all sheer excitement, reminiscent of Long John Silver and Huck Finn, with a dash of ol' faster-than-a-speeding-bullet Superman thrown in for good measure.

At last, the day arrived when I was to take my test to become a Tsunami Ranger. For months, I had prepared by sprinting on the beach, weight training, meditating, and, at every opportunity, paddling out into the sea to learn its lessons. Skirted into my kayak, I learned to breathe deeply in those last, heart-stopping moments before a big wave broke over me, disciplined myself to relax and conserve energy when my boat tumbled end over end in whitewater, and honed my Eskimo roll until it was a split-second, reflexive movement. By examination day, I was as ready as I would ever be.

I arrived at Commander Eric Soares's beach house at the appointed hour. Already present were Captain Jim Kakuk, senior officer of the Rangers, and Michael Jeneid, a photojournalist and former commando in the Royal Marines, who was doing a story on the Rangers. Captain Jim lost no time in leading our party outside and on a vigorous climb up a steep bluff. He paused on a promontory thrusting out high above the beach, where an inspiring panorama of windswept sky and sea unfolded before us. Even at this height, the surface of the sea looked pretty wild that April morning.

The Ranger officers began firing questions at me in rapid succession: "Estimate the wind speed and direction, the swell size and frequency." "What is the tide doing?" "Do you detect any evidence of strong currents or rip tides?" "How would you describe paddling conditions on the reefs below?" Abruptly, Eric and Jim resumed running uphill, with me racing behind. I was panting wildly by the time we arrived at the top, where the cliffs dropped more than 100 feet to the rock-strewn shore below. An ancient cypress tree hung out over the edge of the eroding cliff. "Climb," Jim ordered. The gnarled old tree creaked in the wind as I struggled upward, but I climbed until only wrist-thick branches and a few wisps of foliage remained above my head.

Back on the beach, we pulled on our wetsuits, and Commander Soares led us in the ritual of prayer that precedes every Tsunami mission. Then he gestured at me to join him in swimming. Out through the caldron of pounding surf that was breaking over the reefs we half-swam, half-crawled. Strong northwest winds the past few weeks had caused the water temperature to plummet, and I felt the numbing cold. I was grateful for the protection of my wetsuit and helmet as we swam and when a breaker sent us tumbling over the jagged reef. We fought for every foot of forward progress, but I knew the ability to swim in surf and rocks was deemed an essential survival skill by the Rangers. The words of outdoor writer and surf kayaker Paul McHugh came to me: "To survive, let yourself grow wise. Pain is just a sign of stupidity leaving your body."

At last we reached deep water beyond the breaking surf, where Jim waited with our washdeck Tsunami boats in tow. Eric and I mounted our crafts, and we threaded our way back through the surf-filled rock garden. In the center of the pandemonium, Jim suddenly went limp and fell from his boat into the frothing water. It was up to me to "rescue" him. I pulled his inert form across the deck of my boat and struggled toward shore. Returning to the melee, I narrowly avoided a collision with Eric's unmanned boat when it came charging in through the shorebreak. Where the heck was Eric? I spotted him floating a few yards farther out, also pretending to need assistance.

(continued on page 102)

(continued from page 101)

My rescue skills demonstrated at last, the Rangers determined it was now time to paddle northward on an exploratory mission, a favorite Tsunami pastime. For the intricate rock garden paddling that lay ahead, I switched to a low-volume whitewater kayak, a Perception Sabre. Jim and Eric would remain in their specially designed Tsunami X-1 Rocket Boats.

The seas were definitely building in size and power now. I was ordered to lead the others back out over the foaming reef. The greater hull speed of the Rangers' long, sleek Kevlar boats gave them an advantage in punching through the oncoming surf, and I worked hard to stay ahead of them.

Just as we reached the exposed, outer fringe of the reef, the first wave of a colossal set of storm swell arrived. All around us, thousands of tons of cascading water were colliding with the shallow bottom. Long after each breaker had hit, rebounding surges kept moving back and forth in all directions. As we turned to paddle up the coast, the surface of the sea reminded me of a herd of wild ponies running panic-stricken toward us before the storm. Our boats were flung first in one direction and then another. Solid rock, capable of tearing a kayak to shreds, burst to the surface where surging water had been a moment before. More than once, I glimpsed an X-1 getting totally airborne when two big waves came together beneath it. Hours slipped away as we played this fascinating, deadly game of cat and mouse, with the sea definitely the cat and us the mice. Then, noticing that the sun was falling low in the western sky, we raced back southward. Nearing the cove where we had launched, we caught a great wave and came hurtling together over that reef a final time.

That evening, we gathered with friends at a little café near the sea. Impassioned toasts were offered to Neptune and Odin, amid much laughter and back slapping. Then Captain Kakuk rose and signaled for order. He and Commander Soares proceeded to deliver an in-depth evaluation of my performance that day in the sea. I was surprised at the things they had noticed in the midst of the chaotic circumstances in which we had paddled. Obviously, the Rangers took this testing of a new Ranger very seriously. But much to my relief, they reported that I had done fairly well. The only fault they found was that in some instances my actions had been a bit more reckless than was necessary. "With all due respect," I replied, "that sounds ironic coming from the Tsunami Rangers, considering your reputation as wild men on the lunatic fringe of the sea kayaking world!" Hearty laughter erupted around the table.

Then Captain Kakuk announced that I had passed my test and was hereby accepted into the Tsunami Rangers, with an entry rank of lieutenant commander. Commander Soares presented me with an official Tsunami hat of camouflaged canvas, complete with the gold oak leaf that signified my new rank. There were warm embraces and more toasts. Even the normally reserved British journalist Michael Jeneid seemed deeply moved by the little ceremony. For me, it was one of life's great pinnacles. I remember feeling grateful to the Creative Power that had dreamed up the sea, the waves, the sky . . . and the Tsunami Rangers.

—Michael

Within an extreme-condition sea kayaking team, *individuality* remains very important. Involvement with a good team should enhance, not diminish, the personal power of each individual, and respect is maintained for each member's unique abilities and interests. Everyone is encouraged to express themselves fully and to try new things that might lead the team in new directions. As with any organization, conflicts might arise within a paddling team, but this is not necessarily bad. By facing and resolving problems, the team can grow stronger and develop a deeper understanding of one other.

Sea Tribes around the Water Planet

Along with the phenomenal growth in the popularity of sea kayaking in coastal regions around the world in recent years, more extreme-condition paddling teams are developing. Hardy and resourceful, they thrive in widely scattered regions, from the mountainous, beautiful coast of arctic Norway to the roadless fjord district of southern Chile. In northern California, where a dramatic Pacific shoreline is doubly blessed by a relatively benign climate, they seem to have proliferated. Force Ten, formed by Steve Sinclair, has followed in the wake of ancient Aleutian otter hunters to explore the convoluted Mendocino shoreline. On the Sonoma coast, a group of giant paddlers known as the

Banzai Bozos goes crashing among the offshore rock gardens. The Tsunami Rangers are headquartered about three hours south of San Francisco by kayak and claim the rugged Lost Coast, Big Sur, the San Mateo coast, and certain secret islands off the coast of Oregon and in the Sea of Cortez as parts of our hard-won territory.

Aboriginal sea tribes were driven by the demands of hunter-gatherer survival to compete fiercely with one another for hunting rights and territory along stretches of coastline where game was abundant. They traditionally located their camps on narrow strips of land between two bodies of water, so they could quickly escape in either direction if a superior force of aggressors should appear. Fortunately, today's paddling teams are free to enjoy each other more. They journey, sometimes great distances, to attend each other's races and festive gatherings; to buy, sell, and trade equipment; and to paddle together on exploratory missions. Most sea kayakers are deeply appreciative and protective of the natural world and the marine environment in particular. They also understand and respect other teams' tribal uniqueness and revel in the company of those who share their passion for adventure in the sea.

The next time you go sea kayaking with your friends, try working more closely together as a team. Engage in paddling adventures that will challenge the individual and teach everyone to cooperate more fully and accomplish objectives. Back on the beach, take a few moments to share perspectives and to evaluate everyone's performance. As team spirit grows, so will the skills and confidence of the individual paddlers, and you may become inspired to create a full-fledged sea kayaking team. Then you will discover that you are part of something special, the generation of new sea kayaking tribes that are emerging along the coasts of our water planet.

Dennis Kuhr

The Tsunami Rangers celebrate their team spirit before a launch.

10 Out There

Like those early hunter-gatherers who ventured into the sea and returned to their camps with vivid descriptions of the mysterious world they had visited, kayakers today carry on a rich story-telling tradition. Whether shared around a flickering campfire at night, spoken to an assembled audience at a sea kayaking symposium, or written down and presented with photographs or drawings, stories pass along knowledge and ensure cultural continuity within the widespread paddling community. Throughout this book, we have shared anecdotes with you that we hope clearly represent our experience with the beauty, passion, and practical aspects of extreme sea kayaking. We conclude with a few more tales, complete with morals, of paddling adventures in that wild world beyond the shore.

My First Kayak Crash

After surfing the mild breaks off Coal Tar Point north of Santa Barbara through the summer months, I decided I was ready for the heavy winter surf that began arriving in January 1980. Arroyo Burro Beach featured a rocky reef bottom where strong, tubular surf was breaking on the morning I showed up alone with my fiberglass Dekadense slalom kayak.

Everything seemed perfect. The 10-foot waves washing through every few seconds were well shaped, and the sun was shining. I was in top shape and felt confident I could handle the big waves raging outside. Though I was still new to the sport, I had the sense to wear a helmet, neoprene paddling jacket, shorts, and booties. I launched but waited near shore for a break between sets before trying to paddle through the surf.

A window opened, and I went for it. I plowed through the first wave after it had broken; then I vectored to the left, punched a second wave just as it was breaking, and clawed over the top of a cresting third. Going into a free fall on the backside of that moving mountain, I sucked air so hard it shrieked through my teeth. But I had broken the wave barrier and made it outside.

A few moments later, I got my breath back and was ready to surf. I could see a crowd of hodads gathered at the beach. "Probably expecting to see a puny kayaker get munched by the mighty sea," I mused. A series of 6-foot waves rolled in, then a juicy-looking 8-footer, but I let them pass. Not big enough. Next came a couple of 10-footers. I wanted to jump on one of them but chickened out.

I got this bad feeling that I should have taken one of those 6-footers. The sea around me started to get jumpy, and my spine began to tingle. I felt nervous and unsure about what to do next. Then the water began to suck out and tractor me out to sea. I glanced back and saw this prodigious, tsunami-like wave bearing down on me. It seemed to come from all sides, converging right where I was. I paddled hard, hoping to punch over the top, but knew I wasn't going to make it past this 20-foot Gargantua. Fear gripped me, but I shook it off. No way would I let myself turn to stone and auger in. So, I spun the nose of my boat around toward shore, committed now to surfing the biggest, baddest wave I'd ever seen.

An instant later a wall of water fell on top of me, hard, and pitched me down head first. I hit the trough at the bottom of the wave, got scooped back up into a banzai tube upside down and backward, and then shot back down again into the foaming trough. I writhed around in the liquid twister like a doomed soul cast into Hell. I sensed my body being wrenched out of my boat, my exposed legs raking across the cockpit coaming in the process. My paddle was snatched away, my helmet torn from my head. Then I felt myself being dragged across the rocky bottom. I jammed my hand into a crevice in the reef and melded my body to the floor. When the wave passed, I shot up to the surface and gasped for air.

I watched the giant wave hit the shore like an avalanche, inundate 30 feet of sandy beach, and detonate into the base of the cliff. Spray shot 50 feet in the air. In the aftermath I spotted my tiny boat dangling 15 feet up the cliff face, speared by an exposed root. I was grateful that it wasn't me crucified up there. I swam through the foam and out of the water. Scrambling up the cliff, I wrenched my boat free, slid back down to the beach, and dashed for higher ground before another rogue wave showed up. Recovering my dignity, I strode past the gawking onlookers without a sideways glance. I tossed my water-soaked, battered gear on the top of my VW Beetle and puttered off, heater going full blast.

—Eric

Eric Soares taking off on a wave at Greyhound Rock.

Old Crow Beach

I had heard of them for months—the nebulous and somewhat mystical Tsunami Rangers—and knew about their dubious exploits . . . changing the course of mighty waves, surfing faster than speeding bullets, and kayaking over rocks with a single bound.

My longtime pal, Glenn "It's-not-my-fault" Gilchrist, promised that I was going to have a fun time on my first Tsunami adventure. We drove for hours to reconnoiter with these legends of the sea. To my surprise, we didn't end up on a sun-drenched sandy beach but, instead, at the top of a rain-drenched, muddy cliff, with Glenn announcing that we must descend. It was about midnight, and the waves pounded ominously on the invisible shoreline below.

"You wanna go d-down . . . there?" I stammered. Glenn ignored my whining and plunged ahead, into the blackness. Resignedly, I followed down the mudslide that Glenn called a trail. I guess it was "a good thing" that I couldn't see where I was going, although it was definitely "a bad thing" when I whacked my head on a wet branch in the dark.

After a few more harrowing minutes, we reached a tiny pocket beach. Glenn uttered a strange squeal, and a similar cry echoed back. It must be them. I couldn't see very well, probably because of the blood running down into my eyes. Two hulking entities approached, greeted Glenn warmly, and looked me over. Somebody shined a light into my face to check how badly I was injured and commented, "Gee, he looks like a Tsunami Ranger!"

I thought, "Oh, boy, sign me up."

A small tent was pitched on a little patch of sand that the thundering surf had not yet overwhelmed. Glenn asked if the tide was rising or falling. Rangers Jim Kakuk and Eric Soares answered in unison with opposite responses. Neither of them reminded me of sea legends but more like street people, unshaven and draped in dark tattered rags that fit them all too well.

Glenn and I had carried only essential supplies and equipment down with us. How the bottle of Old Crow whiskey appeared, I do not know. In the pouring rain, Glenn and I pitched our tent in the small space left between the crashing surf and the vertical rock wall. I asked Glenn if this was the fun he had promised. Glenn said, "Yeah, but not as much fun as when the tide rises."

I said, "Great, what's a tide?"

It was difficult to sleep wondering when a large wave was going to claim our tents. As we passed the bottle of Old Crow back and forth between the tents in celebration of our uncertain future, we became steadily less concerned about the approach of the crashing waves.

Amazingly, we survived the night. For breakfast we had—cigars. During breakfast, it was decided to carry the kayaks up the precipice, rather than Jim and Eric paddling them back to the put-in.

I was mildly disappointed that these prodigal Sons of Neptune were not going to demonstrate their kayaking prowess for us in the surf. I was even more distraught when it was decreed that Glenn and I would carry the kayaks up to the road above. Furthermore, the cliff turned out to be covered with poison oak. Of course, that poison oak wasn't here last night!

Glenn and I clawed our way up the trail, clinging to kayaks with one hand and exposed roots with the other. Glenn assured me that our heroic efforts would be looked upon favorably by the Tsunami Ranger elite. At the road, Jim bade a warm farewell to Glenn, thanking him for all the help. Eric turned to me and demanded, "Do you have any food in the car?"

I can't wait for my next Tsunami Ranger adventure. Maybe, if I'm lucky, I'll actually get to see some kayaking next time.

—Dave Whalen

Bob Stender

Dave Whalen, ready for adventure.

Let Eric's story be a warning to anyone thinking about going out in winter surf alone. If Eric had taken a few minutes to study the wave action before plunging in, he probably would have reconsidered. The people on the beach may not have been able to save him, even if they had the skill, equipment, and courage to try. Eric should have sought out a more protected break where the surf was more matched to his skill level. Finally, because of his inexperience, he let himself get caught inside the surf zone by that big wave, instead of immediately paddling out to deep water where it would have been safer.

"Old Crow Beach" is spun by Dave Whalen about his first encounter with the Tsunami Rangers back in 1987.

Gordon Brown surfs a
big one at Easter Island.

Paddling around Easter Island

*By midday the winds had risen to near gale strength and
seemed to be increasing. Looking back at the rugged coast of
Easter Island, I felt the stinging force of the rain on my face and
realized that retreat back the way we had come was no longer
possible. Every few moments an enormous breaker would explode against the steep cliffs bordering this side of the island and
rebound back into confrontation with the oncoming swells. Each
time two waves converged beneath us, we would be lifted high
above the surrounding water, and from there we caught glimpses
of foaming waves spreading all the way to the horizon. Above
our heads, runoff from an antarctic storm was sending tons of
mud and rock washing down the steep flanks of Rano Raraku
Volcano. If an oncoming wave were to break outside and drive us
shoreward, there would be no escape.*

*The storm was pushing us rapidly toward the southeastern tip
of the island, where surf was building up against a lava reef extending far out into the sea. We knew we had to avoid that reef.
Yet to be blown away from this island, the most remote inhab-
ited spot on earth, would be a fatal mistake, too. We allowed the
wind to sweep us a little farther away from the raging shoreline,
until the outline of Rano Raraku became indistinct in the rain-
filled atmosphere. Even here in deep water, the surface of the
sea was convulsive. We passed the tip of the island and turned
north, into an ocean of whitewater. The steep seas were behind
us now, lifting the tails of our kayaks high in the air. Once when
two waves collided nearby, I saw my partner, filmmaker Gordon
Brown, hurtle by inside a 15-foot wall of translucent water. The
words of Michael Graber, director of the ESPN show we were
making, came to me: "Remember, you are not expected to do
anything you consider personally dangerous."*

*At last, we reached the lee side of the island, and things began
to settle down. Just ahead was Anakena Beach, where the Poly-
nesian king Hotu Matua first landed with 100 loyal followers after their long journey from the Marquesas Islands some 1,500
years ago. For us it was a peaceful conclusion to the tumultuous
circumnavigation of Easter Island. Seven silent moais, the gigantic stone statues that Hotu had erected there, gazed out to sea
in greeting. Other words came to me, written by Pablo Neruda,
Chile's Nobel Prize–winning poet, when he visited Easter Island:
"On Isla Pacua, don't trap me. There's too much light, you're too
far away, so much rock and water, too much for me."*

—Michael

By the way, Dave actually got to join the
Tsunami Rangers kayaking the next time
and made the first of lots of silly mistakes
that have become his paddling trademark.
But Dave never gave up, and in 1988 passed
his officer test and was awarded the rank of
lieutenant in the Rangers.

Back to the story. It seems that Dave
had unrealistic expectations of Jim and Eric
on that first encounter. Unexpected things
just happen on extreme-condition kayaking
excursions. By being prepared for the
worst, you will always make it through
the night.

Then there's the "rest of the story,"
told in "Paddling around Easter Island."
Michael did get trapped inside the lava reef
by a big breaker and injured his ribs. The
lesson? A single moment of inattention can
result in disaster. Michael was fortunate to
receive medical assistance in such a remote
spot in the middle of the ocean.

Next is a classic Tsunami Ranger adventure, demonstrating many of the principles
described in this book. As you read it, see if
you can determine what we did wrong—
and right.

Won't Come Back from Gothmog's Churn

The old fisherman in the wheelchair warned that a 40-knot wind storm was blowing down from Oregon, and we could look forward to 10-foot seas. "Groovy," I replied. Jim Kakuk and I jumped on our laden boats and paddled across the mouth of Tomales Bay at dusk. We camped under a full moon at Avalis Beach and were greeted by a herd of elk foraging at dawn.

We launched after breakfast, dodged 10-foot breaking waves while rounding Point Tomales, and turned south toward Point Reyes. We got a fear-laced thrill when 20 feet of blue-eyed, beaked whale, complete with huge dorsal fin, broke the surface and passed right between us. Paddling in waters where great white sharks frequent makes one a bit twitchy when anything big and gray shows up.

After an easy 6 miles in following seas, we landed near Elephant Rock and made camp. From our rocky perch, we gazed straight down into the maw of Gothmog's Churn, a U-shaped cliff face that entrapped advancing waves, causing 40-foot spumes to rise into the air. Long after dinner, we sat watching the action, devising a way to get in there and conquer the churn without paying too high a price. We jokingly sang, "Won't come back from Gothmog's Churn" and hit the hay at midnight so we'd be fresh the next day.

The next morning, to get psyched up for the churn, we paddled over to the double arch at Elephant Rock. Just as we got there, an 8-foot wave picked me up and drove me back toward Jim, who was trying to get lined up to get a picture of me under the arch. I heard him yell "Whoa!" so I flipped over instantly and thrust my paddle down deep into the water to put the brakes on. I missed Jim by inches. Placing another boat between you and breaking surf is what Michael calls the matador style of photography.

Thoroughly warmed up now, we paddled back to the churn and scoped it out for a while. We noted an escape chute near the south end of the churn, where we could haul a boat out in case of a mishap. The sets generally consisted of one or two 10-footers, followed by a bunch of smaller waves. A safe spot the size of a walk-in closet was located in the middle of the churn. The paddler needed to get there when a big wave rolled in, or risk getting bashed into the rocks. We rated Gothmog's a Class 5. You would have to make a lot of ninja strokes to stay in the safety zone and not get creamed.

Jim generously volunteered to take pictures while I made my debut in Gothmog's Churn. I tightened my protective gear, sprinted into the safe zone during a calm moment, and flashed Jim the "thumb's-up" signal. I played with a few 6-foot waves. No trouble. Then I glanced up and saw three 10-footers lining up outside like British red-coats. Three oh-my-god Bagwans were standing up, ready to charge in. "Holy shi-booty," I cried and braced myself for the triple whammy.

The shibooty hit the fan. The first Bagwan broke right in front of me and swept me to within inches of the cliff. Oh well, we anticipated this. All I had to do was get back to the safe zone before that next wave hit. There was a slight glitch, however. The first wave lingered high upon the rock face, holding me there, far too close for a first date! I narrowly escaped the kiss of death by turning my bow toward the sea and sneaked into the safe zone.

The arches of Elephant Rock.

Jim Kakuk

Extreme Sea Kayaking • Out There

Jim Kakuk

Eric Soares in the suckhole at Gothmog's Churn.

Wham! The second diplodicus hit, drove my paddle shaft into my nose, and hurled me upside down into the cliff face. I thought, "This is not good or bad, it's ugly."

Meanwhile, Jim furiously snapped photos of the ordeal and reflected, "I will get rich, rich, fabulously wealthy with these shots."

Once again, the cliff face was ambient with my bleeding face. "We must stop meeting like this," I mused. Then I remembered the Third Wave. Forget heroics. Time for the squirmin' hatch-blower routine. I unbuckled my seat belt and dove for the bottom of the hole. You may wonder how I could submerge wearing a PFD. Well, that water resembled Mr. Bubble in Paul Bunyon's Jacuzzi. I disappeared beneath the foam for a long time, and Jim was growing concerned for the boat. I finally surfaced, swam over to the boat, and shimmied through the escape chute.

Jim seemed shocked by my bloody appearance, but I gave him another "okay" sign and then indicated that now it was his chance to paddle in the churn. He declined, so we wandered into an adjoining rock garden where I spotted an 8-foot rock I could climb to photograph him doing tricks. Luckily, I kept on all my protective gear.

Jim signaled that he was going to punch through a 12-foot wave building up outside. The wave hit, and I managed to squeeze off one quick shot before I was sent flying through the air. I landed helmet first on a barnacle barrio and bounced back into the water. My 8-foot rock had been no match for that 12-foot wave. Jim signaled, "Did you get the picture?" I nodded, "Yes." He paddled closer and chuckled, "While you're swimming around, might as well get some shark's-eye-view shots of me."

—Eric

What did we learn from this adventure? First, that it's possible to combine a kayak camping tour with high adventure. One procedure we used that proved its worth was to establish camp before committing to whitewater extremes and then to venture out in unladen boats. Once again, we were shown how crucial it is to stay within one's skill level while paddling in exposed areas on a most unfamiliar coastline. Risking bodily harm by paddling into Gothmog's Churn was definitely pushing the envelope. We were a long distance from help, if anything had gone wrong.

Another thing we did right was to warm up and tune in before paddling into a challenging situation. We also checked out the churn carefully before entering, making sure we had established a safe zone and an escape route. Ideally, we should have worked out a rescue system before proceeding. We did use hand signals, which enabled us to stay in communication. But what about our plan to _conquer_ the churn? Looking at the photos a few days later, it was obvious that Gothmog's Churn had thoroughly conquered us. Jim had blown two rolls of film, and I had used up two of my nine lives. But it was well worth it.

"The Launch," written by John Lull, highlights viewpoint, communication, rescue, and teamwork.

The Launch

It was so windy that I was concerned my boat would blow off the car rack on the way to the rendezvous at Pistol River Beach on the coast of southern Oregon. But it didn't. While eight of us Tsunami Rangers packed our kayaks on a windswept beach, Dave Whalen's weather radio confirmed the conditions we could see all too well with our own eyes: northwest wind to 35 knots with stronger gusts; seas 10 to 12 feet. A passerby shook her head and suggested we were out of our minds. I briefly entertained the thought that she might be right, but then dismissed it. We were, after all, paddling downwind.

There were a couple of problems, however. After crossing a lagoon, we would have to portage our heavily loaded kayaks about 50 yards across an exposed strip of beach, launch into a heavy surf zone, and make it around the rocky point (called the Gauntlet) to the south. We could see huge waves crashing there, creating a great welter of whitewater. Worst of all, we would have to do all this in howling wind with little or no chance of communication once on the water.

We discussed two strategies. The first was to punch straight out through the surf zone, turn south and paddle around the point. The second was to stay inside the surf zone (in the soup), paddle south along the shore, and look for a sneak route through the rocks. We chose the latter course because it would be easier to land quickly if someone got in trouble.

We launched, one by one, in a predetermined order. Eric and Michael were paddling fully laden doubles (Tsunami X-2s) single-handedly; Jim Kakuk and Bill Collins shared an X-2; Bonnie Brill, Dave Whalen, and James Brooks were paddling X-1s; I was paddling my closed-cockpit Coaster. The order swiftly turned to chaos once we were on the water. Big breaking waves and 35-knot winds tend to screw up the best laid plans.

After launching into the surf, I realized that, as usual, the waves were even larger than they had appeared from on shore. I followed Eric and Bonnie on a parallel course with the shore, fielding the breakers as best I could. Bonnie capsized and swam a couple of times but valiantly recovered and continued on. Because Eric and I were looking after Bonnie (what gallantry!), Jim, Bill, and James moved ahead of us, southward toward the wind- and wave-lashed point. Michael decided to flee the surf zone and paddled farther out to sea. We wouldn't see him again until evening. Dave paddled back and forth between the surf zone and the rocks, until we lost sight of him.

Eric, Bonnie, and I communicated by ESP and stayed together as we drew nearer to the point. Then we saw that Jim, James, and Bill had landed on a small beach inside the rocks. We joined them, thinking this might be our campsite for the night, and had a powwow regarding what to do next. There were two fairly clear passageways out through the rocks, but the interaction of the strong surge-induced currents, vicious wind, and large, unpredictable waves crashing through made both of them look scary.

Then we spotted Dave signaling to us from a bluff further south. If he could make it, so could we. I launched behind Eric and Bonnie. Eric was trying to decide between the two passages when a huge wave crashed through the left passage. That made my decision easy. I headed for the right passage. Eric yelled at Bonnie to follow me. As I fought my way out, climbing up and over progressively larger walls of water, it occurred to me that this would be a very bad scene if one of these foaming monsters decided to break. Moments later I looked up about 15 feet into the crest of a huge curling breaker. The wave was starting to break on my left, so I angled right and clawed up the face. I barely made it over, only to be confronted by another wave, and then another. . . .

Finally, I made it through the Gauntlet and out into the open sea. Now, it was just a matter of clearing the rest of the point in oversteepened, chaotic 12-foot seas. Then a sudden thought occurred to me: what about Eric and Bonnie? They had been right behind me and had to break through the same big waves that I did. I looked back and saw that they had made it out, but I soon lost sight of them as my attention returned to the task at hand. I turned downwind and rode the waves past the rocks at the end of the point. Surfing huge seas with the wind howling and spray flying is an exhilarating sensation, which can only be appreciated through direct experience.

After rounding the point, I spotted Dave in the relatively protected waters on the lee side of the Gauntlet. The group rejoined and we flew south with the wind. Thus began a week of kayaking, camping, and revelry.

—John Lull

Paddling out from the Pistol River launch, we committed a few potentially serious errors in judgment. The first was to launch at all in such powerful winds and gigantic waves with laden boats and at least one inexperienced paddler. Our second mistake was staying inside the soup zone and getting hammered viciously, instead of just powering through the surf as Michael did and running with the wind. We had to battle through the surf zone a lot longer the way we did it, and the rocky Gauntlet was probably the toughest place to punch outside. I guess we thought we were better paddlers than we really were. Luckily we all made it, but it could have been a really bad scene.

Communication between us fell apart quickly in those extreme circumstances. The conditions were so bad that even hand signals failed to keep us in touch with each other. We had agreed to a plan, but that fell apart as soon as we got on the water. We had no backup scheme. Michael abandoned the plan completely as soon as we got in the surf zone. Once he got a clear look at those waves breaking on the point, it seemed right to avoid them by moving out into deep water. It probably was. Dave followed Michael, and we gave up hope of staying together. So much for teamwork.

Bonnie had to be rescued three times in the shorebreak. Fortunately, she made it through the Gauntlet on her own power, but once we reached the big seas outside the surf zone, her fear returned. By then there was no turning back. She gritted her teeth and made it, but she needed some support during the 5-mile paddle downwind to the protected campsite.

Once Michael had battled through the surf with his heavily laden double, he had

Bad Day at Black Rock

"SHARK!!" the divers were shouting. *"There's a shark behind you!"*

John Lull, Tracy Tingle, and I ignored the divers' flailings. We couldn't quite make out what they were yelling anyway, and we never saw the 14-foot white shark that stuck its head out of the water just behind us at Black Rock.

A few months later, we had another scary experience at Black Rock. I took my hard-body, rock-climbing friend Tim Forsell out to Black Rock in my Tsunami X-2 to piddle-paddle around in a partially submerged geosynclinal reef zone. Tim, a novice paddler, had declared he wanted to overcome his nagging fear of the ocean. In my best Alvin the Chipmunk imitation, I responded, "Okay!"

Eric Soares and Jim Kakuk at Black Rock.

We practiced paddling in synch and did a few dump-and-recover routines. Tim struggled at first to reenter the washdeck boat. Instead of "climbing out of the pool" with a scissors kick and mount, he tried "climbing the cornice" with his feet. Typical rock climber move, I thought. Eventually, he got the remount maneuver down.

I suggested we try threading the surf needle at Black Rock and then paddle a couple of miles offshore to enjoy the view of Mount Montara. Tim naively accepted. We headed toward the surf zone. Seven-foot waves were breaking across the reef ahead of us. We passed over a set of small waves without effort. Then a bigger set of waves moved in on us. "Let's go," I said.

(continued on page 112)

(continued from page 111)

Tim made fast movements, but with no real power in his strokes, and wheezed, "I'm pumped."

We barely made it over a 5-foot wave. I yelled, "Paddle faster and harder, Tim!"

"I'm pumped, man," he whined, and flailed at the water. We made it through another wave, but our forward momentum was stalled.

I thought, "For a person who's so pumped, he's acting mighty pooped." I asked what he meant by pumped.

He replied, "I'm . . . exhausted."

An 8-foot comber crested up before us, and I sighed, "Oh shi-booty." The wave broke over us, capsizing the boat, which then rolled over Tim. We both came up gasping, and I yelled, "Get in the boat!"

He was barely able to remount. A moment later, another wave hit, and we capsized a second time. I got back in and told Tim to do the same. He climbed the cornice again and got nowhere. He finally crawled aboard. We were 10 feet from safety, and the same distance from the jaws of death at Black Rock. A tiny wave rolled beneath us, and poor Tim fell out of the boat once more. "Ahh, shibooty," I repeated.

There was no way Tim was going to make it back up again. I had my hands full controlling the boat in the roaring, swirling vortex and couldn't help him much. He started to whimper, and his eyes were glazed. I jumped out of the boat to assist him. More big waves were coming, and I was concerned that Tim might really buy the farm if he got driven into Black Rock. I pushed him underwater just as a wave hit, so the boat wouldn't land on him again. Another Ranger, John Dixon, had been watching us. He pulled alongside and hoisted Tim back into the X-2. John stayed with us as we fled the Black Rock surf zone, just before a 9-footer roared in.

We made it to shore and tended to Tim, who was in shock and hyperthermic. The thick wetsuit, hood, and helmet I loaned him had actually made him overheat with all the exertion. I pulled off his helmet, loosened his wetsuit top, and splashed sea-water on his face and chest, even though it was raining lightly. For a half hour we watched over him while his heart pounded like a taiko drum. We took him home, soaked him in a lukewarm hot tub, and fed him chamomile tea and barley soup. Tim recovered, but he never, ever, went kayaking again.

—Eric

little choice but to just go for it. He remembers the wind being so strong that he had to lean into it and grip his paddle very tightly. "Each time a wave lifted me up out of a trough, the wind slammed into my starboard side like a wall of water," he reported later. "It was a time of absolute concentration, mixed with prayer." Hours before everyone else, Michael reached Cathedral Cove, a secret Tsunami camp-site protected by a maze of sea stacks and arches. We had always approached there from the south before, never from the north. He lit a fire as a signal to us and to warm our bones when we finally arrived.

In years of gnarly ocean kayaking, we've never had a closer call than that one with Tim at Black Rock. We learned that even a gung ho athlete paddling in a double kayak with an ostensible expert can get in trouble in extreme conditions. There was definitely a communication problem over the word *pumped*. To surfers, it means *stoked*, ready for action—yet to a climber, it meant *pooped*, all tuckered out. That misunderstanding almost had serious consequences. Tim and I had practiced reentering the boat before venturing into the surf zone, but that didn't help him much in a crunch. We also learned that a wetsuit doesn't guarantee total protection from the elements.

In retrospect, it was probably foolhardy to take a novice kayaker "through the needle" at Black Rock. Still, we've taken other beginners there, in similar conditions, without mishap. What made the big difference in this instance?

Tim's "latent fear of the ocean," which he wished desperately to overcome, undoubtedly intensified the crisis that developed. We should have paid closer attention when he admitted, "I'm afraid." About a year later, we spoke with Tim again about the incident. He realized then that the *dynamic* danger of the ocean was far different from the *static* danger he was accustomed to on a mountain. Conditions in the surf zone seemed chaotic to him and just overloaded his senses. Ultimately, his mountain-climbing skills and experience didn't transfer to extreme sea kayaking.

Once again, it was demonstrated how quickly a fun paddling adventure can become dangerous, whenever human beings venture out into all the raw power of an exposed coast. Sometimes factors like fear, miscommunication, and questionable judgment interact and intensify a situation. One more time we pondered, what could we have done better?

The Sea Beckons

We hope these tales will inspire you to get out soon in a good kayak and experience the splendor of the ocean environment yourself. But as you can see from our stories, breaking waves and rocks can be demanding teachers, so those who dare to venture out must be well prepared. The benefit of learning vicariously from stories instead of directly from experience is that you can gain understanding from a bad situation without having to suffer consequences. As Bismarck said: "Some learn from experience. I prefer to learn from others' experience."

We've shared what we've learned about paddling in extreme conditions. You, like us, are free to choose your own way in the pathless sea. There are

Kayakers in foldable boats enter a spectacular fjord near the southern tip of South Georgia Island in Antarctica.

Eric Soares

Jim Kakuk slips through crystal clear water off Montserrat Island in the Sea of Cortez.

no traffic cops, streetlights, or signposts out there to tell us when, how fast, or where to go. We hope that this book will help you select the right gear, acquire the essential skills, and prepare for the challenges that await you, out there where few others dare to go. A lifetime of adventure is waiting, just beyond the ragged edges of our water planet.

"What wild, pristine coast calls out to be paddled next?" That's a favorite query among extreme-condition paddlers around flickering campfires late at night. For years, Michael has been planning a Tsunami Ranger excursion across the Bering Strait from North America to Asia with a fleet of ocean-going triple kayaks. A TV documentary about the expedition would focus global attention on this extraordinary wilderness region and would encourage the formation of a proposed international park.

Allison Chase

Michael Powers among the Spitsbergen Islands in Arctic Norway.

114

Eric dreams of circumnavigating the Azores, the islands of his ancestors. Michael and his wife, Nani, look forward to resuming their exploration of the 1,000 miles of wilderness coast and fjords that comprise the southern third of her homeland, Chile.

Any sea kayaker fortunate to live within striking distance of an expanse of open coastline is assured of limitless adventure. Northern California's often volatile interaction with the tempestuous Pacific offers some of the most beautiful and challenging paddling in the world. Legendary Mavericks, where humongous storm swells arrive each winter, lies within sight and easy paddling range of the Rangers' Miramar Beach headquarters. Two hours south in Big Sur, the Santa Lucia Mountains tumble dramatically into the sea. To the north, hundreds of miles of rugged shoreline lead to the enchanted Lost Coast.

Adventuresome, skilled sea kayakers are uniquely privileged to be able to travel freely around this water planet and to explore wilderness areas inaccessible by other means. If you, too, feel a passion for adventure with these swift, agile crafts of ancient design, we heartily encourage you to continue evolving your skills and practical knowledge of the sea. The rewards are unfathomable.

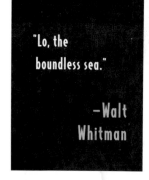

"Lo, the boundless sea."

—Walt Whitman

Tsunami Rangers prepare for their next adventure.

Kayakers negotiate brash ice in a fjord in Tierra del Fuego at the southern tip of Chile.

Kayak Brother

He was drawn to the sea
like a child to Great Mother's knee

For years he lingered by her shore
entranced by her power and learning her lore

Then one fateful day he beheld
A swift, primal form by the waves propelled

There a kayaker danced, fearless and free
calling his land-locked soul to the sea

He sought and soon found
a noble craft with which to bound

Away, at last, from that ancient shore
into a world that promised more

Unseen, within the great surging sea
a kayak brother came to be

Out there, among the waves and the sky
he found others called by the Spirit's cry

Strong, wild and free they were
Life's storms and adventures did they endure

Until at last Kayak Brother grew old
felt in his soul a new longing grow bold

Then one day when all his clan
by the shore were gathered as sunset began

He walked to the sea with a gaze sublime
slipped into his kayak that final time

Without fear he sped from land
straight toward a wave so great and grand

Great Mother came, wall of thundering water
rushing to meet he who sought her

Where they met, the wave suddenly parted
and through the gap his kayak darted

To those who loved him on the shore
came a cry of freedom, then no more

Even now, from time to time
when the waves grow great and green as lime

He can be seen, far, far out there
all sinew and strength and glistening hair

Paddle flashing in the sun
a kayak brother, second to none
 —Michael Powers, Bolinas, California, 1986

Dennis Kuhr salutes
the setting sun.

Resources

The best way to learn how to paddle in extreme seas is to go out there and do it. Yet, we both learned a lot about kayaks and kayaking by reading. Since kayaking on the exposed coast is so complex and risky, take the time to learn all you can before you venture into unprotected waters. Here are some resources we recommend.

Books

Bascom, Willard. *Waves and Beaches: The Dynamics of the Ocean Surface.* Garden City, NY: Anchor, 1964 (currently out of print).

Broze, Matt, and George Gronseth. *Sea Kayaker's Deep Trouble: True Stories and Their Lessons from* Sea Kayaker *Magazine.* Edited by Christopher Cunningham. Camden, ME: Ragged Mountain Press, 1997.

Bunnell, David E. *Sea Caves of Anacapa Island.* Santa Barbara, CA: McNally & Loftin, 1993.

———. *Sea Caves of Santa Cruz Island.* Santa Barbara, CA: McNally & Loftin, 1991.

Burch, David. *Fundamentals of Kayak Navigation.* Old Saybrook, CT: Globe Pequot Press, 1993.

Dowd, John. *Sea Kayaking: A Manual for Long-Distance Touring,* rev. ed. Seattle: University of Washington Press, 1997.

Dyson, George. *Baidarka.* Edmonds, WA: Alaska Northwest Publishing, 1986.

Forgey, William W. *Hypothermia: Death by Exposure.* Merrillville, IN: ICS Books, 1985.

Foster, Nigel. *Nigel Foster's Surf Kayaking.* Old Saybrook, CT: Globe Pequot, 1998.

Hutchinson, Derek C. *The Complete Book of Sea Kayaking,* 4th ed. Old Saybrook, CT: Globe Pequot Press, 1995.

———. *Derek C. Hutchinson's Guide to Expedition Kayaking: On Sea and Open Water.* Old Saybrook, CT: Globe Pequot Press, 1995.

———. *Derek C. Hutchinson's Guide to Sea Kayaking.* Old Saybrook, CT: Globe Pequot Press, 1990.

———. *Eskimo Rolling.* Camden, ME: Ragged Mountain Press, 1992.

———. *Sea Canoeing.* London: A. & C. Black, 1976.

Jeneid, Michael. *Adventure Kayaking: Trips from the Russian River to Monterey.* Berkeley: Wilderness Press, 1998.

Kampion, Drew. *The Book of Waves: Form and Beauty on the Ocean.* Niwot, CO: Arpel, 1989.

Nealy, William. *Kayak: The Animated Manual of Intermediate and Advanced Whitewater Technique.* Birmingham, AL: Menasha Ridge Press, 1986.

Nordby, Will, ed. *Seekers of the Horizon: Sea-Kayaking Voyages from Around the World.* Old Saybrook, CT: Globe Pequot Press, 1989.

Seidman, David. *The Essential Sea Kayaker: A Complete Course for the Open-Water Paddler.* Camden, ME: Ragged Mountain Press, 1992.

Magazines

Canoe and Kayak Magazine
    Kirkland, WA
    425-827-6363

Paddler
    Eagle, ID
    703-455-3419

Sea Kayaker
    Seattle, WA
    206-789-9536

Information on Kayaking in Northern Norway

Crossing Latitudes
    Tim and Lena Conlan
    800-572-8747
    www.mcn.net/~crosslat

Norwegian Tourist Board (**NORTRA**)
    212-885-9700 (New York office)
    www.norway.org

Nordland Reiseliv (official tourist agency
    of Nordland)
    Postboks 434
    Storgt 4a III
    N-8001 Bodø
    Norway
    47 + 755-24-406

Products

Tsunami Kayaks
    Jim Kakuk
    13732 Bear Mountain Road
    Redding, CA 96003
    530-275-4313
    www.tsunami-kayaks.com

Tsunami Rangers Videos
    Eric Soares
    P.O. Box 339
    Moss Beach, CA 94038
    650-728-5118
    The Adventures of the Tsunami Rangers; Kayaking Ocean Rock Gardens; Kayak Magic; The Guide to Ocean Adventure Kayaking; and John Lull's *Surf Kayaking Fundamentals*

Adventure Travel Companies Offering Sea Kayaking Trips

Mountain Travel Sobek
    6420 Fairmount Ave.
    El Cerrito, CA 94530-3606
    888-687-6235
    http://www.mtsobek.com

Wilderness Travel
    1102 9th St.
    Berkeley, CA 94710
    800-368-2794
    http://www.wildernesstravel.com

Index